Final Cut Pro
POWER
SKILLS

WORK FASTER AND SMARTER IN FINAL CUT PRO 7

LARRY JORDAN

Final Cut Pro Power Skills: Work Faster and Smarter in Final Cut Pro 7
Larry Jordan

Peachpit Press
1249 Eighth Street
Berkeley, CA 94710
510/524-2178
Fax: 510/524-2221

Find us on the Web at www.peachpit.com
To report errors, please send a note to errata@peachpit.com
Peachpit Press is a division of Pearson Education
Copyright © 2010 by Larry Jordan

Senior Editor: Karyn Johnson
Copy Editor: Liz Welch
Production Editors: Cory Borman, Hilal Sala
Compositor: Kim Scott, Bumpy Design
Proofreader: Scout Festa
Indexer: Jack Lewis
Interior Design: Kim Scott, Bumpy Design
Cover Design: Charlene Charles-Will
Cover and Interior Illustration: Mark Matcho

ISBN-13: 978-0-321-64690-3
ISBN-10:   0-321-64690-8

9 8 7 6 5 4 3 2 1

Printed and bound in the United States of America

To the readers of my Final Cut Studio newsletter
who provide the incentive for me to keep learning new things every month

Contents

Introduction

I love this book.

Well, OK, I wrote it, so you might consider me a bit biased, but the reasons for my fondness may not be what you expect.

As an editor and a businessman, I've discovered that there is never enough time to get everything done that I need to do. If I can learn a skill or shortcut or technique that can save me a few seconds here and there, that means a lot.

Video editing, even with the best software, takes a long time. And time is a precious commodity.

So the goal for this book is to show you ways you can do things: faster, better, or different so you can get more work done in less time with more fun.

I've been using, studying, and writing about Final Cut Pro for years. This book is a collection of the best of what I've learned. Hundreds of the best time-saving techniques, hidden secrets, keyboard shortcuts, new features, and darn cool stuff for Final Cut Pro that can save you hours of time on each project. (Not to mention slowing your heart rate, decreasing your stress level, and increasing your level of fun.)

If you enjoy puttering, don't read any further.

But if you need to solve a problem, find a way to do something faster, or better, or discover something you didn't know, this book is designed for you. Best of all, you don't need to read it cover to cover—just open it to any page and you'll be saying "ah-HA!" in no time.

This book isn't a textbook. I don't pretend to cover all the features of the application. There are many excellent books that introduce you to Final Cut Pro. Instead, my book takes over where these books end. This is a book for someone who wants to learn Power Skills that the textbooks don't have the time to cover. I'll take you deeper into the application, past the surface, and let you tap into the power of the program.

What this book covers

I've been writing about Final Cut Studio for years in books and newsletters. My monthly newsletter—now in its sixth year—is the oldest and most widely read publication on Final Cut Studio (www.larryjordan. biz/newsletter). Each issue contains more than 35 pages of detailed techniques, along with extended questions and answers with readers from all over the world. These Power Skills are drawn from this extended dialogue each month.

While this book covers the latest version of Final Cut Pro (that would be version 7), many of these techniques—I would guess as many as 75 percent—apply to earlier versions of the software. So, regardless of which version of Final Cut Pro you're using—HD, 5, 6, or 7—this book has something in it for you.

I've organized this book into eight chapters grouped by subject, and then loosely grouped the Power Skills in each chapter by how they relate to one another. However, this is not a novel; you don't read it for the plot. Feel free to dip in anywhere—later chapters don't require you to have read the earlier chapters to understand what's going on.

Each Power Skill is about a single page long and covers a single point. This makes each one easy to read and absorb. Most of them also include a screenshot, which I have carefully designed to show you how to accomplish a task. In most cases, the screenshot answers how, or where, because it doesn't help reading about this great shortcut if you don't know where to click your mouse to create it.

Also, many of these Power Skills include extra information—Extra Credit or Notes—that amplify the skill or show you how it applies in different situations.

My greatest concern in writing this book is that I would miss something obvious. And I may have missed your favorite Power Skill. If you have a technique that has helped you in your work, and you'd like to share it with others, email me at Larry@LarryJordan.biz. I can publish it in my next newsletter, or add it to the next edition of this book.

Where the images came from

One of the hardest challenges in creating a book is finding the right media to use to illustrate the concepts I'm trying to teach. This makes me especially grateful to the following people for allowing me to use their images:

Standard Films and Mike Hatchett for the snowboarding footage.

Dr. Vint Cerf and Alcatel/Lucent for their gracious permission to use video from a speech Dr. Cerf gave in September 2004.

Lisa Younger and Andrew David James for their work on a green-screen project shot specifically for this book.

Jody Eldred for sharing elements of his LAPD helicopter footage.

I'm also grateful to Pond5.com, an open marketplace for stock video footage, who provided additional footage used for this book. They have more than 150,000 clips, very reasonably priced, with more arriving every week. Check them out at www.pond5.com.

Thanks to Brian Greene and Greene HD Productions (www.greenehdtv.com) for permission to use a still from his *Moscow on Ice* program.

Resmine Atis, my actress niece (www.imdb.com/name/nm1742686/), for her stunning head shots and modeling of a Civil War–era dress.

Special people to thank

A book is not created in a vacuum, and there are a number of people I want to thank.

First is my editor at Peachpit Press, Karyn Johnson. This book is her idea and I appreciate her enthusiasm, her patience, and her unyielding opposition to bad writing.

Next is Aleesa Adams, a video editor in her own right, who reviewed each of these skills in their rough draft and made countless suggestions on wording and organization that was invaluable to me in creating the finished version of this book. I am very grateful for her time and her thoughts.

Hana Peters served as production assistant, helping me gather these ideas from a wide variety of sources and get them organized in one place.

Debbie Price, probably the finest executive assistant who ever lived and the person who makes it possible for me to run a company.

My wife, Jane, for patiently allowing me to escape my dinner dishwashing duties for days as I was writing this book.

Most importantly, though, are the readers of my monthly newsletter. I get hundreds of e-mails every day, filled with questions, ideas, suggestions, and thoughts from editors all over the world.

My newsletter grew from these conversations. I learn more each month from my readers than I could possibly fit into each issue. For your questions, advice, corrections, support, and enthusiasm, I am deeply, deeply grateful.

This book was written because of you.

CHAPTER 1

Optimizing Your System and Final Cut Pro

The best way to prevent problems and to achieve maximum efficiency in Final Cut Pro is to set up your system properly. In this chapter, you'll learn how to organize your projects like a pro. Next, we'll walk through key preference settings. I'll also provide media management guidelines for maximizing your storage space.

Then, before we jump into the program itself, you'll learn how to monitor your hardware, explore playback options within the Timeline, and learn key troubleshooting tips to keep everything running smoothly.

These Power Skills will make a world of difference at keeping you and your system editing quickly and smoothly.

Organizing Your Files

You can store files anywhere, but here's a system that's both easy and sensible.

Final Cut Pro is designed so that you can store project files anywhere, but the media that goes into the project needs to be stored and not moved once you've put it in your project. Here's a system that has worked well for thousands of editors. I've modified this slightly to account for the proliferation of servers and external RAIDs.

Final Cut Pro uses two basic types of files: media files that play back natively and files that need to be rendered in order to play back. Media files include video and audio. Files that require rendering include Motion and LiveType projects, Photoshop documents, still images, and so on.

Consequently, I create three folders on my system, with very specific names:

- FCP Projects
- Final Cut Pro Documents
- Final Cut Media

The *FCP Projects* folder can be created and stored anywhere. (I used to suggest keeping this on the boot drive, but it makes more sense to move this over to a second, media drive. The precise location of this folder—boot drive, server, or media drive—is not particularly important.) In this folder, store all the files related to your project that don't contain timecode. (This includes Final Cut Pro, Motion, Soundtrack, and LiveType project files, other audio clips, still images, Photoshop documents, and so on.)

The *Final Cut Pro Documents* folder you create and store is only on separate media drives, *never* the boot drive. This is the folder you point scratch disks to within Final Cut because this is the folder it uses to store all media and render files.

The *Final Cut Media* folder is new. As we increasingly move to tapeless media or creating files in After Effects for Final Cut, we need a place to store those files. That's what I use this folder for.

In the Project and Media folders, you can create whatever subfolders are needed to help you organize projects. I leave the contents of the Documents folder alone.

Back Up, Back Up, Back Up
The worst words you will ever hear are "You've lost all your data."

No one ever believes me when I tell them to work out a backup strategy before they start capturing their first piece of media—that is, until they erase that one critical shot they need for their project. Then, they turn into believers.

Especially today, as we move out of tape into tapeless media, backups become even more critical because you no longer have your source tapes to return to.

Here are three suggestions to consider as you create your own backup system:

1. Use the Autosave Vault built into Final Cut and be sure it stores its files to a *different* drive from the one you use for your project files.

2. Make backups of your project files daily. I tend to make daily backups to a separate hard drive and weekly back-ups to CD.

3. Make sure your media files are stored in at least two different physical places. Hard disks are the best choice for media backups during a project, but should not be used for long-term archival storage.

● **EXTRA CREDIT**

RAIDs (Redundant Array of Inexpensive Drives) are becoming increasingly afford-able for video editing. Keep in mind that low-cost RAID 0 devices are very fast and inexpensive; however, they do not provide any protection in the event of a hard disk failure. RAID 5 devices, though they cost more, provide high-speed data access with the ability to restore your data in the event you lose one drive. RAID 6 devices do everything a RAID 5 device does, plus they can restore your data in the event you lose two drives at the same time. Keep this in mind as you plan your own backup strategy.

● **NOTE**

A quick definition: backups are not archives. A *backup* is something you do during the production process to guard against accidentally erasing a file. An *archive* is something you do when the entire project is complete so that you can modify that project at some point in the future. Hard disks are fine for backups. Digital tape (such as Linear Tape Open, or LTO) is a much better choice for long-term archives.

Creating a File-Naming Convention That Works
The key to successful editing is getting, and staying, organized.

There are as many different organizational systems as there are editors—or, at least, it seems like it. As Mark Raudonis of Bunim/Murray Productions said, "If you can't find a file, you can't work. Period."

Or, as John Gallagher, a reader of my newsletter, wrote: "When it comes to my physical possessions, clothes, etc., I'm really quite messy, but on my computer I tend to be a bit more anal and I just can't stand badly made filenames."

When I get a new project, I create a job code consisting of four characters. First are two letters for the client code (i.e., Just-a-Moment Productions becomes *JM*) followed by two numbers (i.e., their first job becomes *01*). Thus, *JM01* is the code for the first job for Just-a-Moment Productions.

I put the job code at the beginning of every Final Cut, Motion, or Soundtrack project file. I also use it as the start of every graphic or Photoshop document filename. That way, if I ever wonder where a file has gone, I only need to search for the job code.

Tapes or cards get labeled similarly—starting with the job code followed by *_01*. The underscore separates the tape number from the job code. Tapes are labeled sequentially in the order they're shot. If I'm doing multiple camera work, I add *A, B, C…* at the end to indicate the camera position: Left = A, Center = B, or Right = C.

Finally, when capturing clips for scripted shows, I identify the clip based on scene and take. However, since most of my work is for documentaries, I always label each clip where someone is talking starting with their last name. That way, I always know who's speaking—even when I leave a project for a while, because the speaker's name is part of the clip name.

● **EXTRA CREDIT**
When working with tapeless media, create a subfolder in your Final Cut Media folder that starts with the job code, followed by a unique number. That way, all tapeless media can be quickly found and sorted by job code—for instance, *JM01_Card01*.

Setting Your Scratch Disk
Scratch disks are critical to Final Cut Pro working reliably.

The Scratch Disk is where Final Cut Pro stores your media. To get the performance and reliability you need from Final Cut, it's important to properly set up a scratch disk to store your media.

First, and most importantly, this disk needs to be a separate drive from your boot disk. It can be an internal, or external, drive but it must be a separate drive.

Create a folder named **Final Cut Pro Documents** on each drive you want to use to store media.

Select **Final Cut Pro > System Settings**, then select the Scratch Disk tab and "point" the scratch disk to the Final Cut Pro Documents folder you just created using the Set command at the top of the screen.

If you're using multiple drives to store media, Final Cut automatically records media to the drive that's the emptiest. This keeps your media stored evenly across all your drives and decreases playback demands on any one drive.

● NOTE

Never use a USB drive for a scratch disk. It isn't fast enough. PCIe connections are the fastest, followed by eSATA, FireWire 800, then, finally, FireWire 400.

● NOTE

Don't partition the boot drive to create a scratch disk. A partition is slower than a dedicated drive and, even if you do partition the drive, the boot drive is the worst place to put it.

Scratch Disks Are Not Project Based
Final Cut Pro's media is system based, not project based. Here's what you need to know.

Probably the most requested feature that Final Cut Pro *doesn't* support is allowing us to change scratch disks when we change projects. However, in Final Cut Pro 7, this is still not an option.

Final Cut expects you to set your scratch disks once, then leave them alone. It stores all your media inside those scratch disks in folders named after each project. As soon as you start changing scratch disk locations, there's a really good chance some of your files will start going offline because Final Cut Pro can't find them.

So, the workflow is simple:

- Set your scratch disks once and never change them.
- When you create a new project, immediately save it and give it a name.
- Final Cut Pro stores all your media, video render files, audio render files, and related media in folders inside your scratch disks. Specifically, captured or ingested media is stored in a subfolder that is named after your project and stored inside the Capture Scratch folder.

● NOTE

Many editors, in an effort to get around this limitation of Final Cut Pro, try to switch scratch disks between projects. The problem with this approach is that Final Cut Pro changes the folders to which it writes media based on whatever project is active in the Browser. As you switch projects, it invisibly switches folders. This often means you are storing media and render files where you don't expect, causing problems with media going offline later.

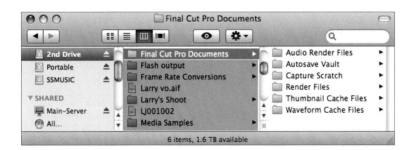

Why Store Media to a Second Drive?

It's all about speed and reliability.

The boot disk has many masters to serve.

The first priority, above all others, is the operating system. When the OS has a question, or needs data, everything else waits while the heads of the hard disk go off to find it.

The second priority, after the operating system, is the foreground application.

After that come background applications.

After that comes data.

But what do we need to play, megabyte after megabyte, minute after minute? Right. Data. However, it has a priority level down near dirt.

So, to solve this problem, we move all our speed-critical media to a second drive—either internal or external.

Now, while the boot drive is going nuts meeting the needs of the OS and applications, our second drive can focus on meeting the playback needs of our media.

● **NOTE**

In a crunch, you can store media to your boot drive. Just remember that this is not the best place for it and will often lead to dropped frames during capture or editing.

● **NOTE**

You tell Final Cut the location of your Scratch Disk by selecting **Final Cut Pro > System Settings > Scratch Disk** tab.

● **EXTRA CREDIT**

In a server-based editing environment, it's often a good idea to minimize network traffic to set render files to a local hard drive, while allowing media files to be captured to a network drive. This provides really good editing performance while minimizing network bandwidth. The only problem with this approach is that render files are stored locally and aren't accessible to other computers on the network.

Configuring System Settings

Of all the preference settings in Final Cut Pro, these are the most important.

There are three preference settings windows in Final Cut Pro:

- **Final Cut Pro > System Settings** configures Final Cut to work with your computer.
- **Final Cut Pro > Audio/Video Settings** configures Final Cut to work with your AV gear.
- **Final Cut Pro > User Preferences** configures Final Cut to work with you.

Of these three, the most important is System Settings.

Final Cut supports up to 12 scratch disks. However, if you need that much storage, you are much better off purchasing a RAID. FireWire is a very chatty protocol. If you connect more than about five FireWire drives, they spend more time talking to each other than transferring data.

In the **Final Cut Pro > System Settings** window, select the Scratch Disk tab. Here, you set scratch disks in the top of the window.

Then, in the middle of the System Settings window you set the location of some technical files. While these can be stored anywhere, I recommend storing them to your first scratch disk. This tends to be both the biggest and the fastest hard drive on your system.

Finally, at the bottom, change the first number, Minimum Allowable Free Space, to **10000**. Hard disks slow down as they fill up. This means that you are always keeping 10 GB (10,000 MB) of free space on each scratch disk.

NOTE

This 10 GB limit has a variety of subtle effects. If you don't have a minimum of 10 GB of free space, Final Cut Pro won't capture, won't ingest, won't render, won't export, and won't print to video. If, during one of these processes, your hard disk exceeds this limit, Final Cut Pro will stop and warn you. In that case, delete some files to make more room so you can continue.

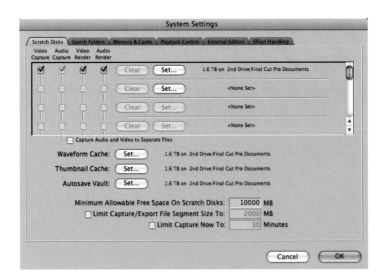

Configuring User Preferences
These preferences tell Final Cut Pro how you want to work.

The A/V settings configure Final Cut Pro to work with your cameras, decks, and tapeless media. Most of the time, the presets are fine. However, these change so quickly it's impossible to cover them in a book. A much better source is Apple's support Web site (www.apple.com/support).

There's one other preference window you need to configure: User Preferences.

The screenshot below shows how I set my system up. While I like the settings for all the check boxes, I dislike the numbers. So here's how I change them.

Final Cut supports up to 99 levels of Undo, but this takes too much memory. A setting of **25** levels of Undo provides a good balance between security and memory.

Autosave Vault is the backup system for your projects. These settings mean it saves every 15 minutes, and keeps the 20 most recent backups from each of the 15 most recent projects.

Auto-Render means that Final Cut Pro will automatically render all open sequences starting 15 minutes after you stop moving the mouse or typing on the keyboard. The best way to enable Auto-Render is to move Final Cut to the background while you work on something else.

● **EXTRA CREDIT**

If you're using a FireWire 400 drive as your scratch disk, select the Limit Real-Time Video option and set it to **22** MB/s. If you're using a FireWire 800 drive as a scratch disk, set this to **45** MB/s. For any other type of drive, leave this setting off.

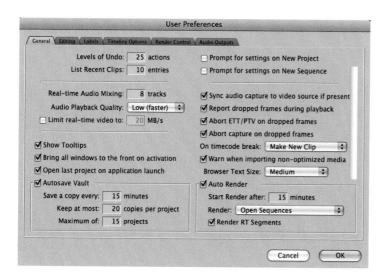

FireWire Tips

FireWire drives slow down your system if you don't pay attention. Here's what to watch for.

Here are some tips for maximizing performance when using FireWire drives:

- A FireWire drive should have at least an 8 MB cache, spin at 7,200 RPM or faster, and use an Oxford chip for data.

- FireWire is very "chatty." The more drives you attach, the more they talk to each other and the less data they transmit. My general rule is to attach no more than five FireWire drives to a system.

- For optimal performance, try not to let hard drives get more than 80 percent full. The emptier they are, the faster they go.

- Keep the *total* length of all FireWire 400 cables to less than 15 feet (5 meters). Longer cable runs have been known to corrupt data.

- Unless you add a separate FireWire card to your system, all FireWire devices are bussed.

This means that the speed of all your FireWire devices is determined by the slowest device plugged in—typically, a camera.

- Connecting a FireWire 400 drive and a FireWire 800 drive into the same computer, either directly or looped through each other, cuts the speed of the FireWire 800 drive almost in half.

- Turn off sleep mode by clicking the Apple icon, choosing **System Preferences**, and clicking **Energy Saver**. Hard disks love to spin and last longer that way, too. For fastest system performance, don't force them to go to sleep.

- When formatting a hard drive, turn journaling *on* for your boot disk and *off* for any hard drive you plan to use for capturing media. Journaling slows media drives down.

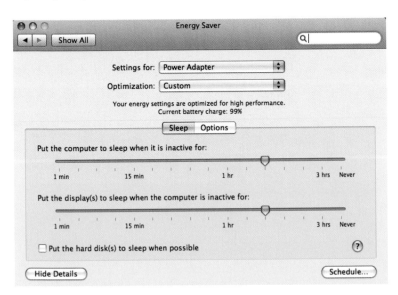

Connecting a FireWire Deck After Starting Final Cut Pro
Here's how to tell Final Cut that you've connected a deck or camera.

Normally, you should turn your FireWire camera, or deck, on before start-ing Final Cut. That way, Final Cut Pro connects to it automatically during launch. However, if you forget, here's what you need to do to get Final Cut Pro to recognize it:

1. Select **View > External Video > Refresh A/V Devices**.

2. Select **View > Video Playback** and set the device you just turned on.

3. Select **View > Audio Playback > Audio Follows Video**, and remem-ber to always monitor audio and video at the same point to avoid sequences sounding out of sync when they aren't.

4. Select **View > External Frames > All Frames**. This sends video and audio to your external device. This includes monitoring, capturing, and output to tape.

5. To test whether you have a good connection, open the Log and Cap-ture window to make sure the "VTR OK" message appears below the Preview window.

Now your deck is good to go.

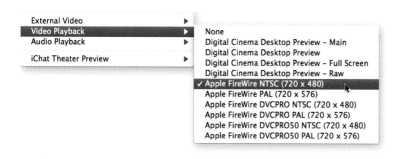

NOTE

When Final Cut Pro starts, it checks to see if a FireWire deck is attached. If it doesn't find one, Final Cut Pro turns off all FireWire input or output for media, which is why we need to go through this procedure.

EXTRA CREDIT

If you don't have an exter-nal video monitor, you can select **View > Video Playback > Digital Cinema Desktop Preview** to turn your main computer monitor into a video monitor. This technique simply makes the picture bigger; you cannot use your unmodi-fied computer monitor for making color or contrast decisions.

Trashing Final Cut Pro Preferences
5 Rules to Trashing Preferences

Final Cut Pro is a very stable program. But, sometimes, it gets confused. Really confused. In that case, the best way to fix it is to trash its preference files.

There are five rules to trashing your Final Cut Pro preferences:

1. Never trash preferences if Final Cut Pro is working properly. Trashing preferences is never needed for maintenance. Never trash preferences "just in case"—only trash them when Final Cut is broken.

2. Only trash preferences after quitting Final Cut.

3. Always trash all preference files as a group. There are four of them and they are linked; don't just trash one or two.

4. Only trash files; never trash folders.

5. Always empty the trash when you are done.

NOTE

There are some great Final Cut Pro preference management programs, which you'll learn about in a few pages.

Trashing Your Preferences

Trashing preferences is a repair procedure. Here's what you need to do.

If you're experiencing Final Cut Pro weirdness or performance issues, try trashing your preferences. Sometimes these files become corrupted and Final Cut Pro loses stability or starts displaying strangely.

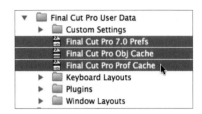

To trash your preferences:

1. Close Final Cut Pro by choosing **Final Cut Pro > Quit**.

2. Open your Home directory (press **Command+Shift+H**).

3. Go to **[home directory]/Library/Preferences.**

4. Trash the file **com.apple.FinalCutPro.plist**.

5. Scroll down to the **Final Cut Pro User Data** folder.

If you're using Final Cut Pro 7.x:

6. Trash the file **Final Cut Pro 7.0 Prefs**.

7. Trash the file **Final Cut Pro Obj Cache**.

8. Trash the file **Final Cut Pro Prof Cache**.

9. Empty the trash.

If you're using Final Cut Pro 6.x:

6. Trash the file **Final Cut Pro 6.0 Prefs**.

7. Trash the file **Final Cut Pro Obj Cache**.

8. Trash the file **Final Cut Pro Prof Cache**.

9. Empty the trash.

● **NOTE**

Be forewarned: when you trash preferences, you'll lose all Favorite motions, transitions, and effects; the list of recently opened projects; and any custom window/button arrangements that weren't saved to disk.

Preserving Final Cut Pro Preference Files

You can preserve or manage preference settings using this software.

The Achilles heel of Final Cut Pro is its preference files. While Final Cut is getting more and more stable with each version, these files still tend to become corrupted on a regular basis. And the only fix is to delete them and start over.

A variety of third-party preference managers are available to help you manage the process. I've used all of these at one time or another and happily suggest them to you:

NOTE

Don't back up preferences until you've created clean files. Otherwise, you'll never know if you are backing up good, or bad, preference files.

- Digital Rebellion's Preference Manager (www.digitalrebellion.com/pref_man.htm)

- Reinphase's Final Cut Pro Manager (www.reinphase.com/en)

- Chesapeake Systems' FCP Attic (www.versiontracker.com/dyn/moreinfo/macosx/32852)

- EditGroove Software's UserMatic (www.editgroove.com)

Here's a secret: Final Cut Pro saves revised preference settings to disk *only* when you quit the program. So, if you're planning to create backups of your preferences, trash them first. Then, go through and create all new settings for everything. Then, quit Final Cut Pro (which updates all your preferences with your revised settings). Since the preferences are brand new, they won't be corrupted. And since you customized them, they're exactly the settings you want to restore in the event of a disaster.

Get Started Faster
Final Cut Pro has two secret ways to start up faster.

Normally when you start Final Cut, the application launches, loads the last saved project you were working on, and displays the sequences you were working on when you last saved the file. This can be very helpful. However, you can override this behavior by holding down the Shift key while clicking the Final Cut Pro icon in the Dock. (Clicking the icon in the Dock is the only way this works.) Final Cut starts but doesn't load any projects. This is a great trick to keep in mind if the last project you were working on takes a long time to load, if you're having problems with corrupted projects, or if you edit a project only once.

Now, with Final Cut Pro 7 there's a second secret key: **Option**.

Normally, when you save your work and quit with a lot of sequences open in the Timeline, they all reopen in the Timeline when you restart Final Cut Pro.

However, if Final Cut Pro hasn't yet started, click to open a project file, then immediately hold the Option key. This opens Final Cut without opening any sequences into the Timeline.

This can often save you time by allowing you to select the specific sequence you want to work on.

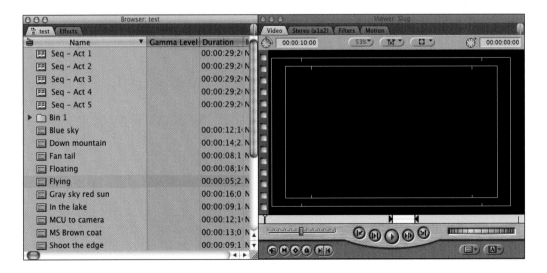

Automatically Launch Final Cut Pro During Startup
You can use this to launch any application when you start your computer.

Here's a fast, automatic way to start Final Cut—or any application—at the same time you start your computer (or when you log in):

1. Select **Apple > System Preferences** and click the **Accounts** tab in the Preferences window.

2. Click the **Lock** icon (in the lower-left corner) to unlock this panel; if necessary, enter your password.

3. Select the Login Items tab and drag the icon for Final Cut Pro (or any other application or file you want to open when your computer starts up) into the window on the right. From this point on, Final Cut Pro will launch whenever you start up your computer.

● **NOTE**

Another way to do this is to Control-click the Final Cut icon in the Dock and select **Open at Login**.

● **EXTRA CREDIT**

To stop a file from launching during startup, simply remove it from the list in this window.

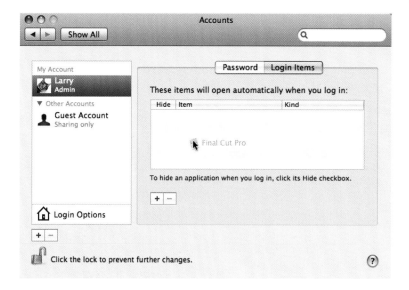

The Benefits of Save As
Save As does more than let you change the filename.

Did you know that **Save As** not only allows you to create a file with a new name, it also fixes internal errors that may be creeping into your Final Cut Pro project? The command also compacts the file, thus removing unneeded internal pointers.

From time to time, make sure you select **File > Save Project As**, give your project a new name, and save it. It's a good idea to use Save As on all your longer-term projects, say every 2 to 3 days.

Keep Project Size Down
Final Cut Pro does not like really large projects.
Here are tips to reduce file size.

Most of the time, Final Cut Pro works fine. However, if navigating around the Timeline starts getting sluggish, you may need to take some preventive measures.

As your Final Cut project grows in size, certain editing functions can slow down. This is normally the result of having too many clips (generally too many clips in the Timeline), using clips with extremely long durations, or using subclips created from clips with very long durations.

To avoid potential performance issues, try dividing long, complex sequences into shorter sequences, and load only the clips for that act into that project.

Also, try capturing in smaller blocks. Long clips can sometimes be a problem, so break a 1-hour tape into shorter blocks, if possible.

Keeping down the clip count and clip duration should help keep Final Cut running smoothly.

● **EXTRA CREDIT**
Project files are generally small. If your project file starts to balloon over 100 MB in size, it runs the risk of corruption. To prevent this, immediately do a **File > Save As** to make a protection copy of your sequence. Then, open the copy and remove as many clips from the Browser as you can to help reduce file size. Once a project file corrupts, it is *extremely* hard to fix.

Understanding the RT Menu
There's RT (real-time) and there's *Unlimited* RT. Here's how to choose.

Tucked into the top-left corner of the Timeline is the RT menu. What the heck does this menu do?

By default, Final Cut Pro plays your images at the highest possible quality during editing; this is the "Safe RT" setting.

> ● **NOTE**
>
> Final Cut Pro always outputs your images at the highest quality; whether to a tape or a file. Here, we are just talking about playback quality during editing.

The benefit of Safe RT is that you always see your images at the highest possible image quality and frame rate, but the trade-off is that more effects need to render.

When you change this setting to Unlimited RT, you are giving Final Cut permission to lower the image quality during editing playback so that it can play more effects in real time.

This is similar to a concept in After Effects, where you can watch your comp instantly in low quality or, after rendering, see it in high quality.

Once you set this menu to Unlimited RT, you can then specify what you want Final Cut to alter: image quality or frame rate.

The *Dynamic* setting means that Final Cut Pro will alter the image quality or frame rate "dynamically," that is, on the fly, during playback. If all you're doing is viewing a clip with no effects, it will play back in high quality. If you're viewing a multilayer extravaganza with 8 billion effects, Final Cut Pro will lower image quality or frame rate, or both, until it is able to play that portion of the sequence in real time.

Most of the time, setting both image quality and frame rate to Dynamic works fine.

● **NOTE**

To work its magic, Unlimited RT does not display everything you have applied to a clip. For instance, it does not display drop shadows, soft or color borders to wipes, or other elements that require heavy processing.

● **EXTRA CREDIT**

For successful multiclip editing and playback, setting this menu to Unlimited RT is essential.

File > Revert vs. File > Restore
Final Cut Pro has a built-in autosave function, but you have to turn it on.

There are two ways you can move back to a previously saved version of your project: **File > Revert Project** and **File > Restore Project**.

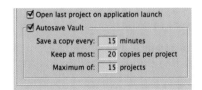

How do you decide which to use?

Revert Project takes you back to the last time you saved your project. You control when and where your project is saved. You also determine what it's called. Using Revert Project means you will lose all changes since the last time *you* saved your file. Revert Project is a good option when you want to return to the last version of your project.

Restore Project takes you back to the last time Final Cut saved your file. Final Cut Pro has a built-in backup system called the Autosave Vault. However, you need to turn it on before you can use it. To do so, choose **Final Cut Pro > User Preferences**, select the **General** tab, and make sure the Autosave Vault option is checked.

● **EXTRA CREDIT**
If you have a corrupted project, you can also use Restore Project to find an earlier copy of your project that works.

Generally, I store the Autosave files on a hard disk separate from where I store my project files. That way, if something happens to my project hard disk, I don't lose both. Also, I suggest you change the default settings to:

- Save a copy every **15** minutes
- Keep at most **20** copies per project
- Maximum of **15** projects

Then, if you forget to save your project and your computer crashes, you can get your project back by choosing **File > Restore Project**. Up pops a dialog box allowing you to select which version you want to open.

Using Render Manager
Here's a great tool for recovering lots of hard disk space.

As long as you don't change the location of your scratch disks, the Render Manager does a great job of tracking your render files.

To use this tool, select **Tools > Render Manager**. The Render Manager window usually has three folders in it: one for the current project, one for all other projects, and Constant Frames, which Final Cut needs. (You may also see render files stored in the Undo Queue.)

Click the disclosure triangle next to the Additional Render Files folder (earlier versions of Final Cut Pro called this folder Additional Projects) to see all projects that have render files. Even if a project is no longer active, its render files probably still exist, taking up valuable hard drive space.

Click the disclosure triangle next to the current project file to see that render files are separated first into sequences, then into audio and video render files.

Don't mess with the Constant Frames folder. It is quite happy being left alone.

To delete render files, click in the Remove column. Final Cut lets you delete render files by type (audio or video), sequence, or project. When you select a file to delete, the total amount of recovered space is shown in the lower-left corner.

Click **OK** to delete the files.

● NOTE

There is no Undo with this tool. So be careful to select the correct project and render files.

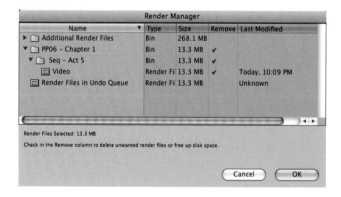

Monitoring Your System
Activity Monitor helps you keep an eye on your system.

Curious to see how hard your processors are working, how much memory your applications are using, or how fast your hard disks are transferring data? Well, you can find all these answers in one place.

Choose **Applications > Utilities > Activity Monitor**. (A fast way to get to the Utilities folder is to press **Command+Shift+U**).

If the Activity Monitor window does not appear, press **Command+1**.

While there are five tabs along the bottom, these three are the most useful:

1. CPU indicates how hard your processors are working. Green dots indicate the amount the CPU is working on your processes, red dots indicate the amount the CPU is working on operating system processes, and black is where the CPUs are kicking back by the side of the pool and waiting for something to happen.

2. System Memory displays four memory states:
   - Wired is memory reserved for, and in use by, the operating system.
   - Active is memory reserved for, and in use by, applications you have started.
   - Inactive is memory reserved for, but not in use by, applications you have started.
   - Free is memory that is not being used.

   If this graph is principally green and blue, you have plenty of available RAM. If it's principally red and yellow, adding more memory may help. (Keep in mind that Final Cut [even Final Cut Pro 7] can only access 4 GB of RAM.)

3. Disk Activity shows how much data is being read (green) and written (red) to your hard disks. This is a fast way to measure hard disk speed, especially if you're getting dropped frame errors.

Isn't it nice knowing these things?

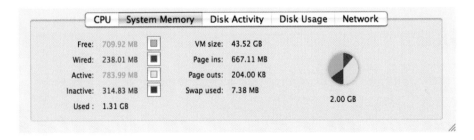

Getting F-key Shortcuts to Work
Final Cut has wonderful F-key shortcuts for editing—none of which work.

Probably the most helpful keyboard shortcuts that Final Cut has are F9 and F10, which quickly perform an Insert, or Overwrite, edit. The only problem is, they don't work. That's because the operating system uses F9 and F10 for things like adjusting audio levels or monitor brightness. Useful, I'm sure, but not to me.

You have two options: change Final Cut Pro or change the OS. Since we know which is the most important application here, we are going to change the operating system shortcuts.

To do so, select **Apple > System Preferences > Exposé & Spaces**. (OS X 10.4 users should choose the **Dashboard & Exposé** preference.)

Click the Exposé tab. Then, while pressing the Control key, reset the pop-up menus for

- All Windows to **Control+F9**
- Application Windows to **Control+F10**
- Desktop to **Control+F11**
- Dashboard to **Control+F12**

What you've done is remap (change) the keyboard shortcuts so they no longer conflict with Final Cut Pro. To call up Dashboard, you now press Control+F12 rather than just F12 by itself.

NOTE

Using Control instead of another modifier key avoids conflicts with other Final Cut keyboard shortcuts.

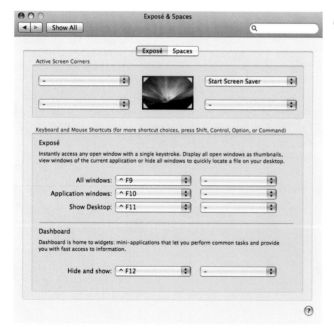

Getting Function Keys to Function
By default, the F-keys on your keyboard don't do what you expect.

Eric Mittan recently e-mailed me about a problem he was experiencing and the solution he came up with. Eric pointed out that on the newest models of Apple's Aluminum and wireless Aluminum keyboards, F9 is assigned to Forward as a media player control button and F10 is assigned to Mute.

Eric wrote, "Now while you can certainly make the argument that a 'real' editor should go out and get themselves a 'real' keyboard, I also think that the budget-minded editor should be able to use the best features of Apple's hardware right out of the box."

So, Eric explained, you choose **System Preferences > Keyboard and Mouse** and click the **Keyboard** tab. Make sure the "Use all F1, F2, etc. keys as standard function keys" check box is selected—this makes F9 and F10 work in Final Cut Pro again.

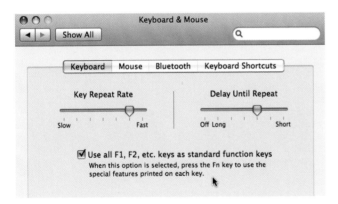

● **NOTE**

The Keyboard and Trackpad window changes depending on your computer and keyboard. Yours may look different.

● **EXTRA CREDIT**

So, how do you use volume controls? Turning on this function disables the functionality of *all* your volume control buttons, not just F10. Note that there is a function modifier key labeled *fn* on the new keyboards. On the wireless aluminum keyboard it's in the lower-left corner of the keyboard next to Control. On the wired aluminum keyboards, it's just under F13, next to Home and above Forward Delete. Press this key in addition to F10, F11, and F12, and your volume keys will function as they did before.

CHAPTER 2

Video Formats, Hard Drives, and Media

Few things in digital media confuse people more than trying to understand high-definition (HD) video formats. Probably the worst decision you can make is to say, "I own this camera; therefore it must be the best one for me to use." As this chapter makes clear, that's a great way to make your life very difficult during editing. Every video format has strengths and weaknesses. Make your selection based on how your project will be viewed, the kinds of effects you need to create, how fast the turnaround is between shooting and final output, and overall image quality.

As you'll discover, learning what these technical terms mean can save you a ton of heartache in the editing suite.

What Do Dropped Frame Errors Really Mean?
It means your hard drive is too slow to keep up. Read on to learn more.

Dropped frame errors are the bane of many editors.

A dropped frame error means that your hard drive is not fast enough to keep up with video playback. This is because not all video formats are the same. Some require very, very fast data transfer rates between the hard drive and the computer. Others are much slower.

There are several ways to solve this problem. The following table illustrates the differences in speed (data transfer rate) based on how you connect your drive to your computer (connection type).

While data transfer rates are generally described in bits per second, I've converted this into megabytes per second (MB/s) to avoid having the numbers get too big.

● NOTE

FireWire is both hubbed and chatty. If you plug multiple FireWire devices into the same computer, the fastest devices slow down to match the speed of the slower device. And FireWire devices spend a lot of time talking to each other. So, the more devices you plug in, the more they chat and the slower your data moves.

DATA RATES BASED ON CONNECTION TYPE

Connection Type	Data Transfer Rate
USB	About 10 MB/s
FireWire 400	20–25 MB/s
FireWire 800	40–55 MB/s
eSATA	75–90 MB/s (laptops)
	120–160 MB/s (towers)
PCIe	175–200 MB/s (laptops)
	275–350 MB/s (towers)

While hard drive speeds continue to increase and variations exist between hard drives, the table on this page illustrates that how you connect your drive delivers markedly different data rates.

There Are Now Five Versions of ProRes
This new codec reduces file size, improves render speed, and maintains quality.

With the latest release of Final Cut Studio (3), Apple released three new versions of ProRes—their high-quality codec for video.

There are now five versions of ProRes:

- ProRes 422 (Proxy)
- ProRes 422 (LT)
- ProRes 422
- ProRes 422 (HQ)
- ProRes 4444

All versions of ProRes support both standard definition (SD) and high definition (HD), at a variety of frame rates, pixel shapes, and image sizes.

Apple describes ProRes as "a variable bit rate (VBR) video codec." This means that the number of bits used to encode each frame within a video stream is not constant, but varies from one frame to the next. For a given frame size and Apple ProRes codec type, the Apple ProRes encoder aims to achieve a "target" number of bits per frame.

ProRes 4444 additionally supports alpha channels—that is, the transparency information in a clip. Apple describes this compressed alpha channel as "mathematically lossless"—meaning it's identical to the original transparency information. If you exclude the alpha channel, there's no difference in *visual* quality between ProRes 422 (HQ) and ProRes 4444.

The only differences between the five versions are the data rates—the lower the data rate, the smaller the file size and the reduced opportunity for image quality. This table shows how Apple describes the quality of the five formats.

● **NOTE**
Final Cut Studio 2 only supports ProRes 422, and ProRes 422 (HQ).

DATA RATES FOR PRORES FORMATS

Codec	Visible Difference (First Generation)	Quality
ProRes 4444	Virtually never	Very high; excellent for multi-gen finishing
ProRes 422 (HQ)	Virtually never	Very high; excellent for multi-gen finishing
ProRes 422	Very rare	High; very good for most multi-gen workflows
ProRes 422 (LT)	Rare	Good for some multi-gen workflows
ProRes 422 (Proxy)	Subtle	OK; intended for first-gen viewing and editing

Different Video Formats Use Different Transfer Rates
Not all video is created equal.

How you connect your hard drive helps determine how fast it is. Here, you'll learn why it matters.

Not all video formats use the same data transfer rate. The following table shows common codecs and their transfer rates. The need for hard drive speed accelerates as you change from SD to HD or add multiple video streams. When editing multiclips, for example, multiply the data rate by the number of concurrent video streams.

COMMON CODECS AND THEIR TRANSFER RATES

Video Format	Average Required Data Transfer Rates (Megabytes Per Second)
SD	
DV NTSC or PAL	3.75 MB/s
DVCPRO-50	7.5 MB/s
ProRes 422	5.25 MB/s
ProRes 422 HQ	7.8 MB/s
Uncompressed 10-bit	26.5 MB/s
HD	
AVCHD	1.5–3.0 MB/s
DVCPRO HD (P2)	15 MB/s
HDV	3.75 MB/s
ProRes 422 (Proxy)*	5.6 MB/s
ProRes 422 (LT)*	12.75 MB/s
ProRes 422*	18.4 MB/s
ProRes 422 (HQ)*	27.5 MB/s
ProRes 4444*	41.25 MB/s
RED (native)	28 or 38 MB/s
XDCAM EX	5.2 MB/s
XDCAM HD (50 mbps)	7.75 MB/s
HDCAM SR	Up to 237 MB/s

*ProRes data rates vary with image size and frame rate. The HD numbers cited here are for 1080i/60; other video formats will create smaller file sizes.

How Much Space for One Hour of Video?
As data rates increase, so does storage.

As you might suspect, as the data rates increase, the amount of hard drive space needed to store one hour of video also increases.

The following table illustrates the storage requirements of different formats. You can use this table to determine if you have enough hard drive space to store an upcoming project.

STORAGE REQUIREMENTS FOR VARIOUS FORMATS

Video Format	Storage Space for 1 Hour of Source Video	Video Duplicated on Ingest
SD		
DV NTSC or PAL	13 GB	No
DVCPRO-50	27 GB	No
ProRes 422	19 GB	No
ProRes 422 (HQ)	28 GB	No
Uncompressed 10-bit	96 GB	No
HD		
AVCHD	Up to 10.8 GB	Yes
DVCPRO HD (P2)	54 GB	Yes
HDV	13 GB	Yes
ProRes 422 (Proxy)*	20 GB	No
ProRes 422 (LT)*	46 GB	No
ProRes 422*	66 GB	No
ProRes 422 (HQ)*	99 GB	No
ProRes 4444*	148 GB	No
RED	137 GB	No
XDCAM EX	19 GB	Yes
XDCAM HD (50 mbps)	28 GB	Yes
HDCAM SR	Up to 834 GB	No

*ProRes data rates vary with image size and frame rate. The HD numbers cited here are for 1080i/60; other video formats will create smaller file sizes.

> **NOTE**
> When working with tapeless media, Final Cut converts some video formats, such as AVCHD, into ProRes 422. The Video Duplicated column indicates where this is the case.

> **NOTE**
> RED footage is a special case. Most often it is not edited in its native format, but uses smaller QuickTime proxy files that point back to the source media. Also, RED files are frequently transcoded to ProRes 422 (HQ).

What Is Bit Depth?

Bit depth determines how accurately we can represent reality digitally.

The world we live in is analog. There's an infinite range of light, color, and sound. However, the computer *hates* infinite ranges. It wants everything reduced to 1s and 0s.

That's where bit depth comes in. Bit depth determines how many steps lie between the absolute lack and the absolute maximum of something—for instance, the number of steps between black and white.

The minimum (black) doesn't change. The maximum (white) doesn't change. What we are varying is the number of steps between them. The higher the bit depth, the more steps, the finer the gradations between steps, and the more accurately we can represent the subtleties in an image.

The Web is 8-bit. Video uses either 8-bit or 10-bit video. While 8-bit is fine for black and white, it tends to display banding on color gradients; 10-bit is better for color, but file sizes are bigger and render times are longer. This table can help you sort all this out.

BIT DEPTH FOR VIDEO FORMATS

Video Format	Bit Depth
SD	
DV NTSC or PAL	8-bit
DVCPRO-50	8-bit
ProRes (all variations)	10-bit
Uncompressed 10-bit	10-bit
HD	
AVCHD	8-bit
DVCPRO HD (P2)	8-bit
HDV	8-bit
ProRes (all variations)	10-bit
RED	10-bit
XDCAM EX	8-bit
XDCAM HD (50 mbps)	8-bit
HD-CAM SR	10-bit or 12-bit

Transfers from film and some digital formats, such as ProRes 4444 (RGB), often use 12-bit depth. This is very useful for high-end digital intermediate work and CGI effects to be projected to a large screen. However, file sizes become extremely large at this setting.

What Does 4:2:2 Mean?

Chroma subsampling determines the amount of color in a block of 4 pixels.

Imagine a block of 4 pixels on your computer. Each pixel has a unique Red, Green, and Blue value. Changing the value of one pixel has no effect on any of the pixels around it. We would describe this pixel block as using 4:4:4 chroma subsampling.

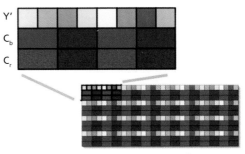

4:2:2 Chroma Sampling

However, most *video* formats don't work at that level of quality. To reduce file size, improve transmission, and just keep things manageable in the past, engineers removed some of the color in a block of 4 pixels. Here's how.

Imagine the same block of 4 pixels, this time on a TV set. Because video needs to support black-and-white images as well as color, we convert the video from an RGB color space to a YUV color space. (Note: It isn't really YUV, though that's what Apple calls it. YUV is for analog video. Digital video actually uses YC_bC_r color space, but, since no one can pronounce that, we'll follow Apple's lead and call this YUV.)

The problem with YUV is that it doesn't contain all the colors inside the RGB color space. Worse, to keep file sizes smaller, some colors get tossed out.

For instance, in 4:2:2 chroma subsampling, we create the same block of 4 pixels. We assign each pixel a unique luminance level (Y). Then, we group the pixels into 2-pixel blocks and calculate an average color for each block. This color can be described using two numbers: hue (the

U value) and saturation (the V value). So, in that 4-pixel block, we have 4 Y values, 2 U values, and 2 V values, which equals 4:2:2.

DV does the same thing, except it creates a single block of 4 pixels, resulting in 4 Y, 1 U, and 1 V, which equals 4:1:1.

For video formats, the highest quality you can get is 4:2:2. However, recently Apple released ProRes 4444. To take advantage of this additional quality, you need to switch out of YUV into RGB—which no video format supports. You would work in 4:4:4 for digital intermediates or high-end CGI work, then convert down to 4:2:2 for distribution on video. For video, working in 4:2:2 is the best choice.

Which Chroma Subsampling Do Various Video Formats Use?

Different video codecs handle color differently.

The following table lists common video formats and the chroma subsampling they contain. You can't change the settings for a format. To improve your color, you'd need to change formats.

If you are shooting pictures with limited effects, any chroma value will look great. If you are doing green-screen work, gradient compositing, or high-end video work for projection, the more color you work with, the better.

CHROMA SUBSAMPLING FOR VARIOUS CODECS

Video Format	Chroma Subsampling
SD	
DV NTSC or DV PAL	4:1:1
DVCPRO-50	4:2:2
ProRes	4:2:2
ProRes HQ	4:2:2
Uncompressed 10-bit NTSC	4:2:2
Uncompressed 10-bit PAL	4:2:0
HD	
AVCHD	4:2:0
DVCPRO HD (P2)	4:2:2
HDV	4:1:1
ProRes 422 (Proxy)	4:2:2
ProRes 422 (LT)	4:2:2
ProRes 422	4:2:2
ProRes 422 (HQ)	4:2:2
ProRes 4444	4:4:4
RED (Native)	4:2:2 or 4:4:4
XDCAM EX	4:2:0
XDCAM HD (50 MB/s)	4:2:2
HD-CAM SR	4:2:2 or 4:4:4

What's Being Dropped in Drop-Frame Timecode?
It isn't what you think.

There are two ways to count timecode: drop-frame and non-drop-frame. While PAL (Phase Alternating Line) editors have never needed to worry about this, NTSC (National Television System Committee) and HD editors do.

One of my favorite questions to my students is, "How many frames of video are being dropped in drop-frame timecode?" It's a trick question. The answer is "none." Drop-frame timecode changes timecode numbering, not video frames.

One hour of drop-frame timecoded video has *exactly* the same number of frames as non-drop-frame timecode video, provided both are running at the same frame rate, such as 29.97 or 59.94 fps.

What's being dropped are timecode numbers. The reason is that NTSC video doesn't run at 30 fps—it runs at 29.97 fps. That 0.03 fps discrepancy means that, over the course of an hour, the actual running time of a tape will differ from the running time displayed in non-drop-frame timecode by 4 seconds and 20 frames.

Drop-frame timecode was invented to fix this problem. It follows this rule: every minute on the minute, skip from timecode 59:29 to 00:02 (thus dropping two timecode numbers) except on the tenth minute, when all timecode numbers are displayed.

This means that drop-frame timecode will display 1:00:00:00, but not 1:01:00:00; instead it displays 1:01:00:02.

Weird but true.

You can toggle between these two settings at any time during an edit by selecting the Timeline and choosing **Sequence > Settings > Timeline Options**.

● **NOTE**

Generally, programs for broadcast, or cablecast, use drop-frame timecode. DVDs, commercials, and films use non-drop-frame timecode. The quality and frame count is identical. What changes is the timecode numbering.

● **EXTRA CREDIT**

While generally considered good practice, the timecode you edit need not match the timecode you shoot. In fact, you can change back and forth between drop and non-drop at any time with no problems.

Defragmenting Your Hard Drive
Once popular, this technique is no longer recommended.

Back in the days of Mac OS 9, we followed the monthly ritual of defragmenting our hard drives. Today, that practice is no longer recommended for any drives that we're using to store media captured, or rendered, by Final Cut Studio.

The reason is fairly simple: When we play video, we don't play it from the beginning of the clip until the end. Instead, we play it from the middle of a clip to the middle of a clip. In others, we play our media in a fragmented fashion.

Final Cut Pro takes advantage of this fact and stores our media in what it calls an "optimized" fashion. Defragmenting a hard drive used to store media, instead of speeding it up, slows things down by removing this optimization.

So, feel free to defragment the boot drive on your computer. Just don't do so with the hard drives you use to store media for Final Cut Pro.

Adding Comments
There are six comment fields per clip—the problem is, most of them are hidden.

When working with lots of clips, it's easy to get lost sometimes—especially when it feels as if you are scrolling forever in the Browser.

Try this simple keyboard shortcut to add comments or a descriptive name to a bin or a clip:

1. Select the bin or clip to which you want to add comments.

2. Press **Command+9**.

3. Click the **Logging** tab.

4. Scroll down until you find the comment field you want to use.

5. Type in the comment that you want, and click **OK**.

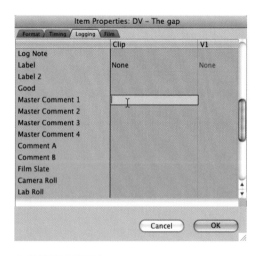

- **EXTRA CREDIT**
  You can search on text contained in Comment fields by choosing **Edit > Find**.

What Are Audio Sample Rates?

Sample rates are used to convert analog audio into digital audio for the computer.

Sample rates are used to convert the infinitely variable waves of audio into something the computer can store. When a microphone "hears" a sound, it converts it into electrical energy. This energy is measured in volts, ranging from –1 volt to +1 volt.

A sample is a measure of the voltage at a particular moment in time. The sample rate determines how many samples are collected each second.

According to the Nyquist Theorem, if you divide the sample rate by 2, you will determine the maximum frequency that a particular sample rate supports. For instance, a sample rate of 48 kHz (48,000 cycles per second) provides a maximum upper frequency of 24,000 (48,000 ÷ 2 = 24,000).

Normal human hearing ranges from about 20 cycles per second (extremely deep bass) to 20,000 cycles per second (extremely high treble). So, a sample rate of 48 kHz yields a frequency response that exceeds human hearing.

Here's a table that can help you pick the right sample rate for your project.

NOTE

Sample rates of 96 kHz and 192 kHz are used in high-end audio post. The ear cannot hear the difference, but the additional data makes a difference when extensive audio processing is anticipated.

SAMPLE RATE FREQUENCIES

Sample Rate	Also Called	Equates To
11,025	11.025 kHz	Poor AM Radio
22,050	22.05 kHz	Near FM radio; best for spoken podcasts
32,000	32 kHz	Better than FM radio
44,100	44.1 kHz	CD audio; best for music
48,000	48 kHz	Standard DVD and video recording; best for music

The higher the sample rate, the higher the potential quality (assuming all other things being equal), but the larger the file size.

One of These Is Not Like the Other
Here's how to tell one clip from the other.

Most of the time, everything works great. Editing is going well, your story is being told. Then, suddenly, poof! Something isn't working.

But where's the problem?

Here's a great diagnostic tool that allows you to quickly compare multiple clips in the Timeline at once.

Select the clips you want to compare and choose **Edit > Item Properties > Format** (press **Command+9**). This opens a window that displays technical settings from all the selected clips. This is essentially the same information that the Browser displays, but in a much more useful format.

Notice that some of the text is gray and some is black. If the text is black, it means the setting for that clip is different from the clip to the left of it. (This is why all the data in the far left clip is black—there's no clip to the left of it.)

If the setting for a clip is the same as the clip to the left of it, the text is gray. This allows us to quickly see which clip is different so we can determine whether that difference is significant. For example, file sizes differ for each clip, which is not an issue. But if the codecs were different, or frame size, or frame rate, this could cause a problem in your sequence.

The cool thing about this window is that it makes finding differences between clips very, very easy.

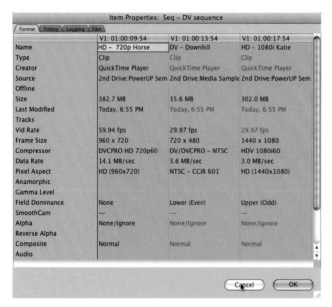

● **NOTE**

The Timing, Logging, and Film tabs contain more information about each clip (and use the same gray/black interface to display data).

Changing a Clip to Anamorphic in the Browser
Sometimes a clip is imported with the wrong aspect ratio. Here's how to fix it.

Sometimes a clip gets imported as 4:3 and Final Cut Pro does not realize that it needs to be 16:9.

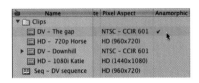

The difference between anamorphic and non-anamorphic video is the shape of the pixel. The total number of pixels in the image remains the same.

Anamorphic pixels tend to be short and fat; 4:3 pixels tend to be tall and thin. The Anamorphic flag in Final Cut Pro simply tells the application what shape it needs to use when drawing the pixels.

NOTE

If you have a single clip you want to change, just click in the Anamorphic column without holding down Control.

If you haven't yet edited the clips to the Timeline, changing the aspect ratio is easy to fix in Final Cut Pro's Browser:

1. Select the clip, or clips, you want to change in the Browser.
2. Scroll to the right in the Browser until you find the Anamorphic column.
3. Holding down the **Control** key, click in the Anamorphic column for a clip you want to change, and select **Yes**.

If you have already edited the clip to the Timeline:

1. Select the clip.
2. Choose **Edit > Item Properties > Format** (press **Command+9**).
3. Scroll down till you see the Anamorphic line and check in the appropriate column.

Changing How QuickTime Displays Anamorphic Video
If your anamorphic videos look stretched, you need to read this.

Anamorphic video changes the shape of the pixels so that, rather than displaying an image as 4:3, it displays it as 16:9.

Something nobody talks about is that anamorphic video has *exactly* the same number of pixels as regular video—it's just that the pixels have different shapes.

Because of this, sometimes when you export a video from Final Cut, QuickTime plays it looking stretched or squished. That's because QuickTime isn't sure what aspect ratio your pixels are in, so it displays your video using square pixels.

To reset how QuickTime displays your video:

1. Open the clip in QuickTime Pro (you need the Pro version to do this).

2. Press **Command+J** (or choose **Window > Show Movie Properties**).

3. Select the Video track near the top of the window.

4. Click the **Visual Settings** tab.

5. Deselect **Preserve Aspect Ratio**.

Then, depending on what video format you're using, enter one of these sets of numbers for Scaled Size:

- DV NTSC 16:9 or PAL 16:9: **720x405**

- 720p HD: **1280x720**

- 1080i HD: **1920x1080**

This makes everything look great again.

● **EXTRA CREDIT**

To improve image quality, also check **High Quality** in the lower-right corner. If you are playing interlaced media, check **Single Field**.

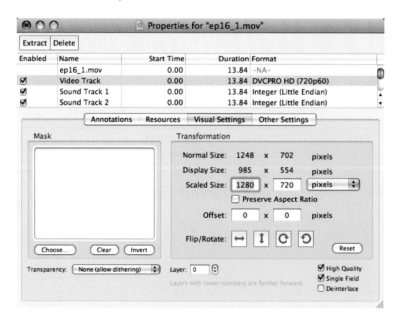

Improve QuickTime Movie Playback on Slower Systems
Here's a codec that plays well on a wide variety of machines.

While H.264 is the star of the codec world at the moment because it creates small file sizes with great image quality, it isn't always the best choice when you want to create a QuickTime movie. Why? Because H.264 requires a seriously fast computer to play back smoothly.

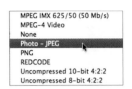

For this reason, if you want to create a movie that will play on older, slower machines, or you want to create a movie that will play without requiring a lot of computer processing power, say for a ProTools session, consider using the Photo-JPEG codec.

It won't create really small files, but it does play back without a lot of stress, even on older, slower systems.

Better Quality from VHS
VHS has never had the best quality—here's how to improve it.

If you find yourself needing to capture from VHS tape from time to time, you may have noticed that the image quality coming off the deck is not exactly pristine. Looking for something you can do to improve your image without spending a fortune?

● NOTE
You don't need TBCs for making digital copies, since a digital duplicate is identical to the master.

Try a TBC (time base corrector). This piece of hardware, about the size of a paperback book, is the answer. A TBC cleans up the video signal so that the picture looks better and is more stable during playback. And it's relatively inexpensive.

TBCs can be rented as part of the VHS deck, or they can be a separate piece of equipment. As an example, see the DataVideo TBC-1000.

You can use TBCs for analog dubs or for capturing directly into Final Cut Pro. In either case, you should notice a marked improvement in image quality.

Looking for a Good Codec for Archiving?
Here's a video codec that's a good choice for long-term file storage.

The problem with almost all video codecs is that they are lossy. That is, a video clip loses quality whenever you record something using that codec, or convert a video clip into that codec.

Most of the time, that loss is not a problem. But suppose you want to store your materials for a long period of time. For instance, say you want to store historical footage from the 1930s. In this case, maintaining image quality with a format that is nonproprietary is critical.

For these situations, consider Photo-JPEG. When the quality is set to 100 percent, the format is 100 percent lossless. Everything you put in stays in. Photo-JPEG is the best nonproprietary codec for retention of quality. Even better, it plays natively in Final Cut Pro.

Avoiding Interlacing Problems

Be careful of flicker when working with NTSC or PAL video.

NTSC and PAL video are both interlaced. So is any HD format that ends with the letter "i"— 1080i, for example.

Interlacing divides the image into alternating sets of lines—odd lines and even lines. It displays the first set, then a fraction of a second later, it displays the second set. Some formats, like NTSC, display the even, or lower, lines first. Other formats, such as HDV, display the odd, or upper, lines first.

For projects destined for television or DVD, interlacing is fine because virtually all TV sets display interlacing in such a fashion that you don't see it. However, interlacing becomes a problem when you output projects for the Web for display on a computer screen, start working with still images, or export freeze frames.

In these cases, interlacing causes bothersome visual anomalies in your video, indicated by thin horizontal lines radiating from all moving objects or wild flickering on still images containing thin horizontal lines.

Here are a few things to keep in mind:

- Freeze frames of moving objects shot with interlaced video always flicker. This is especially noticeable on computer screens.

- If you need to deinterlace within Final Cut Pro, choose **Effects > Video Filters > Deinterlace**. The default settings of this filter are fine.

- When compositing two images, if both are interlaced and both are scaled to 100 percent, be sure they align on even lines using the Motion tab (it's the right-hand number for the Center parameter).

● **EXTRA CREDIT**

To keep confusion to a minimum, Final Cut Pro hides interlacing by displaying just one field at any time. If you want to see interlacing, set the magnification of either the Viewer or Canvas to **100 percent**.

A Fast Way to Convert from One Video Format to Another

Here's the world's fastest way to convert to a new video format.

You've been editing happily in [insert the name of your video format here]. Suddenly, the client calls up and says they need a copy of your sequence in [insert name of any other video format here that is totally incompatible with what you are doing now].

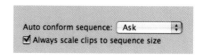

Clearly, the very first thing you should do is hang up the phone and swear at the client. However, while this will make you feel better, it won't really help the situation.

Here's what you do:

1. In your current project, choose **Final Cut Pro > Easy Setup** and select the video format the client needs.

2. Create a new sequence. (You must do this *after* you've changed the Easy Setup.) Double-click it to load it into the Timeline.

3. Go to your existing project, select all your clips by pressing **Command+A**, and choose **Edit > Copy** (press **Command+C**).

4. Select your new sequence. Put the playhead where you want your clips to start and choose **Edit > Paste** (press **Command+V**). If a dialog box appears asking if you want to change the sequence settings, click **No**.

Done. This won't be the absolutely highest quality; Compressor provides better quality. But this method is very, very fast.

● **EXTRA CREDIT**

There is a preference setting in Final Cut that has an impact here. On the Editing tab in User Preferences, be sure the bottom-right option is set to **Ask** or **Never**. Using **Always** resets the sequence settings to match your clips. Also, be sure "Always scale clips to sequence size" is checked. Otherwise, your clips won't resize properly.

When Do You Need an Alpha Channel?
And what *is* an alpha channel, anyway?

The alpha channel is that portion of an image that contains transparency information. The red channel holds the settings that determine how much red is in each pixel. The green and blue channels do the same: they determine how much green and blue is in each pixel.

Well, the alpha channel is a fourth channel that tells each pixel exactly how transparent or opaque it is. (Life would be much simpler if the folks who invented television would have called it the transparency channel—but they didn't.)

The new version of ProRes 4444, which Apple calls ProRes 4x4, uses RGB color space (which isn't used in video but is used in computers for digital effects). ProRes 4444 also has the option to add an alpha channel to the red, green, and blue information. Hence the four 4's—red, green, blue, and alpha.

If all you're creating is full-screen video, you'll never need the alpha channel. But if you're creating a video clip that needs to fill only a portion of the screen—say a company logo or some text animation—then you need to use the alpha channel.

Only three video codecs support alpha channels:

- TGA, also called Targa files, which is principally used for image sequences.
- Animation, the long-time go-to format when alpha channels are needed.
- ProRes 4444, the new kid on the block in Final Cut Pro 7.

If you have the option to use ProRes 4444, use it. It has higher quality with a smaller file size than the older Animation codec. Otherwise, for earlier versions of Final Cut Studio, Animation is your best choice.

Black and White
4 Grays
4 Colors
16 Grays
16 Colors
256 Grays
256 Colors
Thousands of Colors
Millions of Colors
✓ Millions of Colors+

● **EXTRA CREDIT**

By default, Final Cut Pro doesn't export alpha channels. To make sure alpha channels are handled properly, choose **Sequence > Settings** and click the **Advanced** button near the bottom. Select **Millions of Colors+** from the Depth pop-up. The plus indicates the alpha channel will be exported.

● **NOTE**

The new Share feature of Final Cut Pro 7 also allows you to export alpha channels when you use the ProRes 4444 setting, but only if you change the sequence settings as mentioned in the Extra Credit, above.

CHAPTER 3

Ingesting Media

Whether you record your images to tape or to flash memory, or draw them with crayons on paper and scan them into a digital image sequence, at some point you need to get your files into Final Cut Pro. That's what this chapter is all about.

You can bring images into Final Cut Pro in one of three ways: capture your images from videotape, transfer them from tapeless media, or import images that the computer can already read, such as Photoshop documents.

This chapter starts by looking at still images—typically a complete snake pit of confusion and conflicting advice. Using the information provided here will make your life a whole lot easier.

Using Cover Flow to Find Shots
Here's a handy way to find stuff fast.

Have you explored how useful Cover Flow is in OS X 10.5 (Leopard) for finding a missing shot?

Adam Lloyd Connell wrote me about this recently: "I am currently working on a long project with around 500 takes, and the cinematographer had only supplied one take of a particular cutaway to an object on a table. Trying to find that specific clip without the continuity notes easily at hand was a pain, and using FCP's thumbnail view was slow.

"However, opening folders with footage from the XDCAM and selecting Cover Flow mode made it so easy to flash past all the hundreds of (quite large) thumbnails, and we found the shot in minutes. I've gotten into the habit of finding my missing shots in Finder this way. Try it next time you're trying to find that elusive shot."

Just open your media folder, select all the images you want to review, and press the spacebar. Ta-da!

Picking the Best Format for Still Images
Not all image formats are created equal.

The general rule for working with still images is to keep them at the highest quality possible at all times. However, not all image formats are designed for high-quality work. Some are designed for very small file sizes, or reduced colors, or even no colors at all.

For instance, JPEGs and GIFs are designed to generate small file sizes optimized for the Web. But the compression they use decreases the quality of the image.

LAB and CMYK images are designed for print work. Final Cut Pro won't even import them.

Others, like EPS, are optimized for maximum resolution, providing extremely high quality with a small file size by employing vector-based mathematics. However, since all video images are bitmapped, this format needs to be converted to bitmaps before it can be used, which reduces the value of using vectors.

Image formats that work best for video are bitmapped, uncompressed, and high quality. The two formats I recommend for single-layer images that don't contain transparency are PNG and TIFF.

If you're creating an image that contains transparency, save it as a PSD.

● NOTE

PICT images, though older and Mac-only, are also fine. There are other image formats that fulfill specialized needs for video editing, such as Targa and DPX files. These are most often used when exporting images from 3D software packages.

Importing TIFF Images in Final Cut Pro
Not all TIFFs are created equal.

When creating images for importing into Final Cut Pro, you can use the TIFF or PNG format. Both are excellent choices.

When saving your TIFF files, be sure to use LZW compression. Files saved using ZIP compression often refuse to import properly into Final Cut Pro.

Also, be sure to save TIFF images using Macintosh byte order. Final Cut Pro has trouble importing TIFFs saved using IBM byte order.

> **NOTE**
> Where possible, avoid JPEGs, as they contain image compression artifacts, which degrade your image.

Stills Don't Have to Be 10 Seconds Long
You can change the duration of imported images. Here's how.

By default, Final Cut Pro imports all still images and creates freeze frames, applying a 10-second duration.

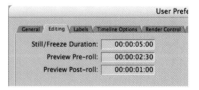

You can change this by selecting **Final Cut Pro > User Preferences**, selecting the **Editing** tab, and adjusting the Still/Freeze Duration setting.

> **EXTRA CREDIT**
> When creating a slide montage, measure the time between downbeats of the music, then change this Duration setting to match that time. This way, all your stills import perfectly timed to match the music.

> **NOTE**
> This setting affects imported image files, including PSDs, and freeze frames that you create in Final Cut Pro. It does not affect any imported video clips.

Sometimes, Mid-Tone Gray Isn't
Mid-tone gray is determined by the gamma setting.
Here's how to set it.

Macs, PCs, and video set the value for mid-tone gray at differ-ent points. This setting is called Gamma (think "G" for *gray* and *gamma*).

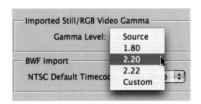

The Mac sets Gamma at 1.8, while PCs and video set it at 2.2. This means that an image that looks perfect on the Mac looks light and washed out in video. Conversely, an image that looks great in video looks dark and muddy on a Mac using standard Mac Gamma.

Final Cut Pro adjusts for this by changing the default Gamma setting to 2.2 while the program is running. Most of the time, that's fine. However, if you import a file that just doesn't look right, you can correct it—either before importing the image or afterward in the Browser.

To set the Gamma setting automatically on import, select **Final Cut Pro > User Preferences**, click the **Editing** tab, and adjust the gamma in the Gamma pop-up menu.

To change the Gamma setting in the Browser, select the clip, and then scroll right until you see the Gamma column head-ing. Setting Gamma to **1.8** will lighten an image; setting it to **2.2** darkens it.

● **NOTE**

File formats for which Final Cut Pro can adjust gamma include JPEG, PNG, TIFF, SGI, PlanarRGB, MacPaint, and layered or flattened Photoshop (PSD) files. It can also adjust gamma for QuickTime movie files compressed using the None or Animation codec.

● **EXTRA CREDIT**

Snow Leopard (OS X 10.6) changes the default gamma setting of your Mac to 2.2. So, this problem essentially goes away once you upgrade.

Playing Still Images in Real Time
You can control how many images play in real time.

One of the exciting challenges in documentary editing is trying to bring a sequence to life when all you have to work with are still images.

Normally, adding a few stills to your sequence causes no problems. But, as you start to add more and more images, real-time playback can suffer.

Final Cut Pro offers a preference setting that allows you to allocate more RAM to your still images. It's called the Still Image Cache and here's how to set it.

Choose **Final Cut Pro > System Settings** and click the **Memory & Cache** tab. By default, Memory & Cache is set to 10%. If you're working with lots of images, bump this up to **15%**, or maybe as high as **20%**. I would not recommend going higher than that.

The size of the still cache is limited by the total amount of unused physical RAM installed in your computer within the standard 4 GB memory allocation used by Final Cut Pro. The larger the still cache, the more still images can be played back in real time in the currently selected sequence.

NOTE
The RAM allocations in Memory & Cache do not need to total 100 percent.

NOTE
If you're working with more than one sequence, whenever you switch sequences, the still image cache switches to the new sequence.

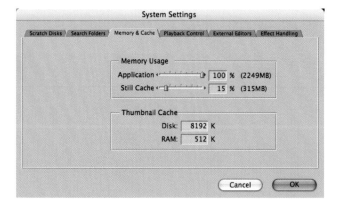

Sizing Still Images for Import into Final Cut Pro
Create images that look good both on the computer and in video.

Nothing drives editors crazier than trying to figure out how to make still images look good. The problem is that video uses rectangles for all its pixel shapes, while computers use square pixels; this is called the Pixel Aspect Ratio.

Hundreds of pages have been written about this, but let's keep this simple. If you are creating a full-screen, still image in Photoshop to import into Final Cut Pro, use the following table.

This table assumes you want the image to display full screen, without transparency, and without movement on the image. To use it, find your video format, pick your aspect ratio, and then create your image to match these specs.

GUIDE TO SIZING IMAGES CORRECTLY

Video Format	Aspect Ratio	Create Your Image At This Size
DV NTSC	4:3	720 x 540
	16:9	853 x 480
SD NTSC	4:3	720 x 547
	16:9	853 x 486
PAL	4:3	768 x 576
	16:9	1024 x 576
HD 720	16:9	1280 x 720
HD 1080	16:9	1920 x 1080

● **EXTRA CREDIT**
Because video uses a fixed resolution for each video format, changing the dpi (dots per inch) doesn't improve your images. Create all images at 72 dpi.

● **NOTE**
Yes, Photoshop has pre-built image aspect ratios you can use to create stills. However, Adobe and Apple calculate the Pixel Aspect Ratio differently. You can use Photoshop's presets, but they're designed for Adobe Premiere Pro, not Final Cut Pro. Therefore, for the greatest accuracy, use the numbers shown here.

Sizing Images for Moves
If you want movement on your images, use this table.

The previous Power Skill provided sizes for still images that won't contain movement.

But what if you want to pan, tilt, or zoom an image? Well, the one thing you *don't* want to do is enlarge any image more than 100 percent. That just makes it soft, grainy, and unpleasant to look at.

Instead, create the image larger than you need so that it gets reduced in size inside Final Cut Pro. That way, your images will have great-looking quality, even when you zoom into them.

The sizes in this table are designed only for single-layer images (TIFF or PNG; PSD images are covered in the next Power Skill). Remember to always create your images at 72 dpi.

These image dimensions will allow you to pan as much as you want and zoom in up to 2.5 times without any loss of image quality.

> **NOTE**
> Use the Scale parameter on the Motion tab in Final Cut Pro to adjust image size.

> **NOTE**
> Final Cut Pro often has problems with images greater than 4000 pixels in size. Keep your image dimensions below this limit if possible.

GUIDE TO SIZING IMAGES THAT WILL CONTAIN MOVEMENT

Video Format	Aspect Ratio	Create Your Image at This Size
DV NTSC	4:3	1800 x 1350
	16:9	2133 x 1200
SD NTSC	4:3	1800 x 1368
	16:9	2133 x 1215
PAL	4:3	1920 x 1140
	16:9	2560 x 1140
HD 720	16:9	2560 x 1440
HD 1080	16:9	3840 x 2160

PSD Images Are a Special Case
PSD images are treated as sequences, not as images.

Sizing single-layer images is easy compared to sizing PSD files. This is because Final Cut Pro imports PSD images containing transparency as though they were sequences. This just confuses everybody because PSD files still use square pixels while video uses rectangles—so after you import the image, it doesn't look the way you expect.

Here's the solution. From the following table, create your image sized from the Master Image Size column based on the video format and aspect ratio you're using. When all the design work is complete, save your file as a PSD. This becomes your "Master" file.

Using this Master file, in Photoshop, choose **Image > Image Size**. Turn **off** Constrain Proportions and then resize the image to the specs in the Squished Image Size column. Save this resized file. This is the "Squished" file that you'll import into Final Cut. Next, and this is a *critical* step, in Final Cut Pro make sure your Easy Setup settings match the sequence you plan to edit this image into. If they don't, your PSD files won't import properly.

Finally, import your images. If you follow these steps, everything will look great.

NOTE

Every video format is different. Unlike single-layer images, with PSD files you need to know the exact number of pixels your video camera is shooting. While this table lists some of the most popular formats, if your camera format isn't listed here, check with the manufacturer for its specs. Use those image size numbers to create the Squished Image Size.

NOTE

Some HD video formats record their images using square pixels; in which case, creating a "squished" version of the PSD file is not necessary.

SELECTING IMAGE SIZE

Video Format	Aspect Ratio	Master Image Size	Squished Image Size
DV NTSC	4:3	720 x 540	720 x 480
	16:9	853 x 480	720 x 480
SD NTSC	4:3	720 x 547	720 x 486
	16:9	853 x 547	720 x 486
PAL	4:3	768 x 576	720 x 576
	16:9	1024 x 576	720 x 576
HDV 1080	16:9	1920 x 1080	1440 x 1080
HDV 720	16:9	1280 x 720	(Not needed)
DVCPROHD (P2) 1080	16:9	1920 x 1080	1280 x 1080
DVCPROHD (P2) 720	16:9	1280 x 720	960 x 720
AVC 1080	16:9	1920 x 1080	(Not needed)
AVC 720	16:9	1280 x 720	(Not needed)
RED 1080	16:9	1920 x 1080	(Not needed)
XDCAM HD 1080	16:9	1920 x 1080	1440 x 1080
XDCAM HD 720	16:9	1280 x 720	(Not needed)
XDCAM EX 1080	16:9	1920 x 1080	(Not needed)
XDCAM EX 720	16:9	1280 x 720	(Not needed)

Working with Long Image Sequences
Too many images gum up the system.

An image sequence is a number, generally a very large number, of still images that you want to build into a movie. They're most often created in stop-motion animation or exported from 3D packages during rendering.

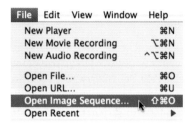

It's a bad idea to load large numbers of individual images into Final Cut Pro. The frames are loaded into RAM, which fills up quickly. Even if you adjust the Still Image Cache setting, it's easy to bring your system to its knees if you're using thousands of images.

Instead, open a long image sequence in Quick-Time Pro by selecting **File > Open Image Sequence**. Pointing to the folder containing your images, open them as a single file.

Then select **File > Export** to export this sequence as a QuickTime movie. For highest quality, set the codec to either ProRes 4444, or QuickTime Animation if you are on an earlier version of the software; or you can match the codec you plan to use for your Final Cut Pro sequence to save rendering time.

A Faster Import
Here's a fast way to import a gaggle of clips into a folder in the Browser.

Yes, you can drag clips from the Desktop into the Browser. But dragging a slew of clips and trying to accurately hit an itty-bitty Bin folder depends too much on my fatigue factor. Instead, my preferred method is to Control-click the Bin in the Browser that I want the imported clips to land in and choose **Import Files**.

In the Choose a File window, you can preview clips and Command-click to select the ones you want. Click **Choose** and all your chosen files show up in the Bin you wanted them to land in. No chance of missing the Bin—slick!

● **EXTRA CREDIT**

You can use this same technique to import an entire folder of files by choosing **Folder**, rather than **Files**, from the Import menu.

Working with PowerPoint Slides
You can easily integrate PowerPoint or Keynote slides into Final Cut Pro.

Need to integrate Microsoft PowerPoint or Apple Keynote slides into a video presentation?

The trick is to create and design your PowerPoint or Keynote slides to match, as closely as possible, the image size of video. For example, with SD, create them at 800x600. For HD, try 1280x720. You'll still experience a loss in quality, because video is lower in resolution than the images you create on your computer, but doing this will minimize the quality loss.

Remind your artists to decrease the amount of text on the slide and make the font size bigger. Also, export the slides as either TIFF or PNG images to get the best quality possible to import into Final Cut Pro.

NOTE

Keynote provides the option of exporting animated slides as video. Exporting as a QuickTime movie makes it easy to create transitions in Keynote, but it exports every slide that doesn't have movement using a duration of a single frame. You'll need to change the duration of this exported frame once you edit the QuickTime movie into Final Cut Pro's Timeline.

Create a QuickTime movie that can be viewed on Macs and Windows computers.

Importing Text for Text Clips

You don't have to type text into text clips—you can import it.

Normally, you create a text clip and type your text into it. But what if that text exists in another file. Can't you just import it?

Well, yes and no.

Let's say you have your text stored in a Microsoft Word document. If you simply copy and try to paste it into a Final Cut Pro text clip, it won't work. That's because text stored in any rich text program like Word has hidden formatting codes embedded into it.

The key is to get rid of those codes before pasting it into Final Cut Pro. Here's how.

After you create your text clip in Final Cut Pro, copy the text from Word and paste it into TextEdit (a simple word processing program that ships with your Mac). TextEdit strips out all the hidden codes and displays just the text.

Next, in TextEdit reselect your text and choose **Edit > Copy** (press **Command+C**). This step is critical; otherwise, the old Word-formatted text is still in the clipboard.

Switch over to Final Cut and paste your text into the Text field for your clip.

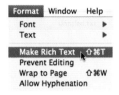

NOTE

TextEdit has two modes: simple text and rich text. For this technique to work, TextEdit must be in simple text mode. You can verify the setting in Text Edit by opening the Format menu. If you see the option Make Rich Text, the file is in the correct mode. If you see the option Make Simple Text, select it to switch formats.

Reconnecting Media
It isn't hard, provided you follow a few simple precautions.

Final Cut Pro is designed so that you can store your project file anywhere. However, Final Cut expects that once you capture, transfer, ingest, or import media, that source file is going to stay put. Even more important, Final Cut expects that you will not rename any files or folders containing files.

If files get moved or renamed, that worrisome red line appears in the missing clip in the Browser and the Timeline displays the red Media Offline warning.

You can reconnect three types of media: offline, online, and render files. First, never reconnect render files. Their naming convention is obtuse beyond words. Just give them up for lost and re-render. Life is too short.

Second, the only reason to reconnect an online file is if, in a fit of editorial passion, you connected the Browser clip to the wrong media file on your hard disk. While not unheard of, this is pretty rare.

Third, and most common, is when a media file gets moved or renamed on your hard disk.

Whatever the cause, select all the Browser or Timeline clips you want to reconnect and choose **File > Reconnect Media**. Here you have essentially two choices: Locate and Search.

Use **Locate** if you have changed the name of the file and *you* need to find it.

Use **Search** if you have moved the file, but not changed the name, and you want Final Cut to find it. Search is *much* faster.

● **NOTE**

Final Cut Pro now uses Spotlight indexes to find media during searches. You'll find this helpful when searching for media stored on servers.

● **NOTE**

Final Cut Pro 7 now sorts clips displayed in the Log & Transfer window to show only the clips that require recapturing. If you have a lot of clips, this can make your screen a lot less messy.

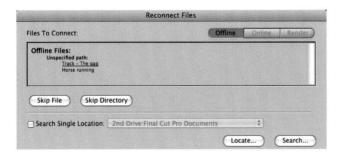

Setting the Reel ID
The Reel ID tracks where your media came from. Here's how to change it.

Whether you're using tape or tapeless media, Final Cut Pro uses the Reel ID to keep track of the source of your media.

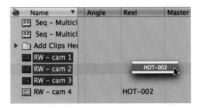

To digress for a minute, there are four key pieces of data that Final Cut uses to link clips in the Timeline and the Browser with the source media on your hard disk: the filename, source timecode, Aux 1 timecode, and Reel ID. Change any one of these and they are changed everywhere—in your project, in your sequences, and on your hard disk.

Originally, the Reel ID linked the box of videotape your media was recorded on with the clip in Final Cut's Browser, which made recapturing clips from videotape possible. Now, with tapeless media, the Reel ID also links to the name of the folder containing your source media. This means that if you ever need to recapture tapeless media, Final Cut will know what folder(s) to look in to find the source material.

You can change the Reel ID in several places. Probably the easiest is the Browser. Select the clip, or clips, you want to adjust, and then scroll right until you find the Reel column.

If the Reel ID already exists, Control-click the column and pick the Reel ID from the pop-up list. Otherwise, just double-click the column entry and type the ID you want to use.

Final Cut displays a warning just to make sure your changes are correct. When you click **OK**, the Reel ID will be changed in the Browser, in every related clip in the Timeline, and in the media file recorded on your hard disk.

● **EXTRA CREDIT**

In addition to changing the Reel ID in the Browser, you can change it by choosing **Edit > Item Properties > Logging** or by choosing **Modify > Timecode**. Wow! What a lot of choices.

Only Capture the Audio Tracks You Need
Select which audio tracks you capture or ingest.

In both the Log & Capture window and the Log & Transfer window, you can specify which audio tracks you want to bring into Final Cut.

In both cases, reducing the number of audio tracks you capture reduces the storage space needed for the file.

In Log & Capture, click the **Clip Settings** tab in the top-right corner.

In Log & Transfer, click the **Import Settings** tab below the Preview window.

Toggling the green visibility light determines whether the audio is captured. In either screen, an illuminated green visibility light indicates an active track that will capture audio. Dark green means an inactive track that won't capture audio.

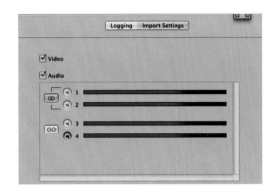

● **EXTRA CREDIT**

To capture your audio as a stereo pair, click the cassette icon to put a bracket around your audio. To capture audio as dual-channel mono, click the cassette icon to remove the bracket. In the screenshot, tracks 1 and 2 are stereo, while tracks 3 and 4 are dual-channel mono. Capturing audio from track 4 has been turned off.

Monitoring Audio During Capture
You are not going deaf—the audio is off by default.

Audio monitoring during capture first appeared with Final Cut Pro 5.

Open the Log & Capture window and click the **Clip Settings** tab. Make sure Preview is checked. This turns on audio play-through during capture.

● **EXTRA CREDIT**

Keep in mind that monitoring the audio during capture adds to system overhead. Occasionally this creates problems in the captured file, usually manifested as random clicking. Where possible, monitor your audio directly off the camera or deck rather than through the computer during capture.

● **NOTE**

The Preview button will be grayed out if you don't have a deck or camera attached to your system.

The Fastest Way to Control a Tape Deck
The world may be going tapeless, but tape decks still exist.

Here's a great little Power Skill that makes controlling a tape deck a piece of cake. When in the Log & Capture mode/window:

- Press **L** to play the deck going forward.
- Press **J** to play the deck in reverse.
- Press **K** to stop playback.

● **EXTRA CREDIT**

If you have an In or an Out set on the deck, you can quickly shuttle the deck to the In by pressing Shift+I, or shuttle to the Out by pressing Shift+O. This also works great in the Preview window of Log & Transfer, too. (Well, it also works in the Viewer, Canvas, and Timeline… but don't tell anyone.)

With that as background, let's see what else we can do:

- Press **L** up to six times to go forward up to six times faster than real time.
- Press **J** up to six times to go in reverse up to six times faster than real time.
- Press **K+L** at the same time to go in slow-motion forward.
- Press **K+J** at the same time to go in slow-motion reverse.

Converting Media
Final Cut Pro does not like compressed media. Here's how to convert it.

Final Cut Pro was designed to work with original source media. It really doesn't like media that's been compressed. For instance, putting MP3 or AAC audio in Final Cut Pro's Timeline often results in audio with clicks, pops, and drop-outs.

Trying to play MPEG-2, or M2T, or other compressed video files will frequently bring Final Cut to its knees. A much better approach is to convert your media into something Final Cut Pro can work with before bringing it into the program.

iTunes is a great conversion utility for audio. So is Soundtrack Pro, or QuickTime Pro. In Soundtrack, open the file you want to convert as an Audio File project. Choose **File > Save As Copy** and select **AIFF** from the Format menu at the bottom.

For converting video, Squared 5 Software's **MPEG Streamclip** is the acknowledged master. You can find the current version of this free utility at www.squared5.com.

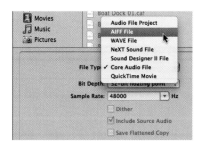

● **EXTRA CREDIT**

Final Cut Pro allows you to mix both 44.1 kHz and 48 kHz audio on the same Timeline, without requiring rendering. However, if you also add 32 kHz audio, Final Cut will need to render it.

Log & Transfer Beefs Up
Working with tapeless media is improved in the latest version of Final Cut Pro.

Log & Capture is how we bring in media from tape. Log & Transfer is how we bring in media that is tapeless. And the latest version of Final Cut Pro has made this process much more robust.

Most times, for safety, we store the original source media on hard disks that are not attached to our computer. That way, we can't erase files by mistake. Final Cut Pro 7 makes it easy to find and mount missing volumes when you need to recapture clips.

In addition, the Logging section has been improved to make it simpler to log clips with an improved naming section.

● **EXTRA CREDIT**

A very cool feature about Log & Transfer is that you can rename any clip and Final Cut will remember the original name of the file. If you ever need to recapture media, you don't need to worry that you renamed your clips prior to bringing them into Final Cut.

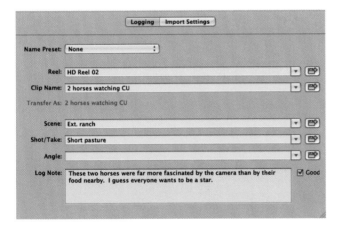

Batch Capturing Media After Disaster
I know you didn't mean to erase your hard disk, but, well, accidents happen.

OK. The worst has happened. Some or all of your media just disappeared. Gone. Permanently. Missing.

Clearly, the first thing you need to do is stand up, swear, and blame the computer. Because this certainly wasn't your fault! However, this is only a temporary solution, because it won't bring your media back.

Recapturing can… provided, that is, you've been obsessive and made sure every clip has a Reel ID—whether tape or tapeless. With the ID, everything is possible. Without it, it's gonna be a loooong night. (If clips are missing a Reel ID, you can still add them, even if they are offline. I covered this earlier in this chapter.)

All the missing clips have a red line through them in the Browser, so select all the clips you want to recapture. These can be from different tapes or folders; Final Cut is really good at tracking all this stuff. It processes tape-based media first, then tapeless.

Choose **File > Batch Capture**. If you need to recapture tape media, the Batch Capture window appears. This is the same window we use during regular capture. The cool part is the next window. This is a list of all the different tapes Final Cut Pro needs to recapture your media. As long as your Reel IDs are accurate, all you need to do is load each tape when Final Cut Pro asks for it, and poof! All your media gets recaptured. (I love watching the computer capture all my clips automatically.)

If you're working with tapeless media, be sure to mount the hard disk containing the source files before starting this process. Final Cut automatically opens the folder in which you stored the original media. (The folder name is used as the Reel ID during transfer.) It asks permission to start, and then pulls all your media back in.

● **NOTE**

Renaming tapeless media is not a problem. Final Cut Pro remembers the original name of the media assigned by the camera during recording. The key is the Reel ID.

Working with AVC Media
A new family of video codecs provides more options.

AVCHD (Advanced Video Codec High Definition) is a video format jointly developed by Sony and Panasonic. There are, currently, three varieties: AVCHD, AVCCAM, and AVC-Intra. The first two use GOP (Group of Pictures) encoding, while the latter uses I-frame encoding. GOP files are smaller, while I-frame files edit without requiring conforming.

Final Cut Pro does not support native editing of AVCHD or AVCCAM. Instead, when you ingest them using the Log & Transfer window, it transcodes (converts) it to ProRes 422. The benefit to this conversion is that ProRes edits, renders, and outputs faster than any GOP-based video codec. Plus, ProRes provides equal or greater quality for clips, transitions, and effects.

● **NOTE**

Once AVCHD or AVC-Intra has been transcoded into ProRes, it cannot be exported back into its original AVC format.

The latest release of Final Cut Pro now supports AVC-Intra video natively. Currently, AVC-Intra is only recorded on Panasonic cameras. Now you have two choices: You can play, edit, and apply effects to AVC-Intra footage natively, or you can transcode during ingest into ProRes 422.

The question of what to do depends on where you want to spend your time. The advantage to working with AVC-Intra natively is that you can ingest quickly and start editing faster. However, you can't export back into the AVC-Intra format, which means you need to transcode into ProRes, or some other codec, during final export.

Transcoding into ProRes takes longer at the beginning of a project, and it also increases your storage requirements because you need to duplicate all the media. However, output is very fast because you don't need to convert the media during export.

Before ingesting AVC-Intra media natively, you need to select the P2 AVC-Intra plug-in. To do this, open **Log & Transfer**, click the small gear to open the preferences window, and select **P2 AVC-Intra** in the Source Format column.

CHAPTER 4

Working in the Application

One thing that Apple is very proud of is the interface for Final Cut Pro. The word *interface*, however, covers a lot of territory. It's what we work in for hours at a time. It's how we interact with our project. And based on how well we understand it, it can determine whether we are happy or frustrated, productive or panicking.

This chapter is filled with dozens of Power Skills you can use to turn yourself into an interface master.

Change the Size of Text in the Browser and Timeline
We can't change the font, but we can change the size. Here's how.

It seems to be an unwritten rule in Apple's interface guide-lines that text needs to be so small and tasteful as to be almost unreadable.

Which is a real problem when you're actually trying to read it.

Not to worry, though, there's a fast solution to tiny text. Control-click in the gray area of the Name column of the Browser and change the text size from **Small** to **Medium** (my favorite) or **Large**.

The text changes size in both the Browser and Timeline. Sadly, this only affects Browser text and Timeline filenames. But even this goes a long way to reducing eyestrain.

● EXTRA CREDIT

You can also change these settings by choosing **Final Cut Pro > User Preferences**, clicking the **General** tab, and using the **Text Size** pop-up menu.

● NOTE

Final Cut will remember these text size settings until you change them, or you trash your preferences.

● EXTRA CREDIT

If you own Final Cut Pro 7, choose **Tools > Timecode** and celebrate that you can finally put your reading glasses away!

Zooming the Timeline
Here's a quick way to zoom the Timeline.

Everyone knows that **Command+=** zooms into and **Command+-** zooms out of the Timeline horizontally.

But what they *really* do is zoom the active window. (The active window is the window that's currently selected.) This often means that when you press these keys and expect to zoom into the Timeline, instead the image in the Viewer explodes into fat pixels! What if you want to zoom into the Timeline and it isn't active?

What we need is another option. This is exactly what I have for you...

Press **Option+=** (Option and the equal key) to zoom into the Timeline. Press **Option+-** (Option and the minus key) to zoom out. These work whether or not the Timeline is selected.

● **EXTRA CREDIT**

In Final Cut Pro 7, there are two new hidden shortcuts, not assigned to any button or keystroke, that allow you to zoom into, or out of, the position of the playhead in the Timeline. To see them, choose **Tools > Button List** and search for "on playhead." These are the two new choices. Skills later in this chapter illustrate how to create custom buttons or keyboard shortcuts for them.

Zooming Faster
There are more ways to zoom than you might expect.
Here's a new one.

So, Option-zooming isn't fast enough for you?

Well, here's a faster way to zoom into anything—if you have the latest version of Final Cut Studio and a late-model laptop that supports multi-touch gestures.

● **NOTE**

Don't have a trackpad? Hmm... then read the next Power Skill.

You can use gestures to zoom in and out:

- Pinch two fingers together on the trackpad to zoom in.
- Spread two fingers apart to zoom out.

The Two Fastest Ways to Zoom
These two keyboard shortcuts do a blindingly fast za-za-zoom.

I use these two keyboard shortcuts constantly:

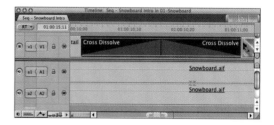

- To compress or expand the contents of any window to fill the window, press **Shift+Z**.

- To compress or expand any *selected* area of your sequence to fill the Timeline window, press **Shift+Option+Z**.

These are flat-out the two fastest ways to zoom in and out that I've ever discovered. Wow!

● **EXTRA CREDIT**

Shift+Option+Z is a great way to zoom into a transition or just a small group of clips. Just select what you want to magnify and press the magic keys.

Vertical Movement
The ability to scroll vertically is built in, but that doesn't mean it's easy to find.

There are multiple ways to scroll vertically in the Timeline in Final Cut Pro. Choose your favorite!

- If your mouse has a scroll wheel, place the cursor in the middle of the Timeline and roll the wheel up or down.

- Drag either of the blue scroll bars, one for video and one for audio, up or down at the right side of the Timeline.

- Use the up and down arrows at the right side of the Timeline.

- Although not technically scrolling, you can grab the heavy, gray bar in the middle of the Timeline and drag it up or down to reveal more or less of either the video or audio tracks.

● **EXTRA CREDIT**

Press **H** to select the Hand tool. You can drag vertically or horizontally in the Timeline to move. This is the only tool that allows you to move both horizontally and vertically at the same time.

Image Quality in the Viewer vs. the Canvas
The two windows don't display the same quality—here's why.

Ever wonder why the same image in the Viewer and the Canvas doesn't look the same?

The image in the Viewer is displayed in its source resolution. The image in the Canvas is displayed based on the codec you've selected for the sequence.

For instance, in this illustration both images are the same TIFF and displayed in both monitors at 50 percent. The sequence is set to DV NSTC 4:3, which, when displayed in the Canvas, definitely has less detail than the source image in the Viewer. This illustrates how the choice of a video codec impacts the detail in your finished sequence.

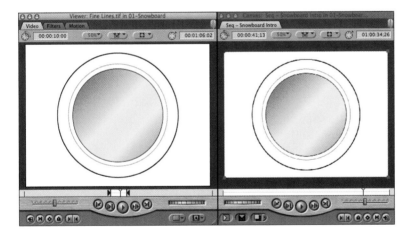

Monitor Your Video Full Screen

Turn your computer monitor into a full-screen video monitor.

First, a very important warning: Using your computer monitor to make color decisions about video can be dangerous because the color, black, mid-tone gray, and white levels of your computer monitor don't match a video monitor.

Given that, there are many times where we want to look more closely at our images. As Academy Award–winning film editor/sound designer Walter Murch once said, "We look *at* television, we look *into* film."

As our images move from SD to HD, there's more detail to examine, and the small Viewer and Canvas screens in Final Cut Pro don't make that detail easy to see.

To turn on full-screen display, choose **View > Video Playback** > **Digital Cinema Desktop Preview – Main**.

Your screen will likely go black and you'll think you've just destroyed everything. Not to panic! Press the spacebar and your Timeline will begin to play—full screen!

To switch back to Final Cut, press **Esc**. To toggle back to the full-screen display, press **Command+F12**. (If nothing happens, it's because the operating system is messing with your keyboard shortcuts again. See page 23 in Chapter 1 to learn how to fix this.)

● **EXTRA CREDIT**

All the keyboard shortcuts you use in the Timeline also work in full-screen mode: J, K, L, Up/Down arrow keys, Left/Right arrow keys, and so on.

● **NOTE**

While this technique works for both SD and HD video, SD will look really grainy when enlarged to fill a large computer screen.

● **NOTE**

If you have two computer monitors, you'll see other choices in the View > Video Playback menu: Preview and Raw. Preview displays video on the second monitor and scales it to fill the screen. Raw displays the video on the second monitor and displays its pixels accurately without scaling, which means it may not fill the frame, or it may be so large you can't see the entire image.

Remove Scroll Bars for Better Playback
Scroll bars cause choppy playback.

Final Cut allows you to zoom into the picture within both the Canvas and Viewer. While this is very helpful for effects work, it is not a good idea for playback.

Even with today's fast machines, Final Cut has problems playing clips smoothly—especially HD clips—when you have scroll bars displayed in either the Canvas or the Viewer.

To solve this problem, select whichever window has scroll bars and press **Shift+Z**. This resets the image size so that it properly fills the window and makes the scroll bars disappear.

Get in the habit of pressing Shift+Z whenever you finish working with an enlarged image, and before starting playback.

Back to Square One
Here's a keyboard shortcut that resets all your windows.

Are you one of those editors who constantly rearranges her window layout while editing? Do you yearn for a quick way to resize your windows back into a layout that makes sense?

Shhh…. Here's the secret: press **Control+U**. This shortcut automatically resets all your windows to the default layout.

Isn't that convenient?

● **EXTRA CREDIT**
You could do the same thing by selecting **Window > Arrange > Standard**. But life is too short.

iChat Theater

Here's a great way to collaborate on your project by sharing the video.

New with Final Cut Pro 7 is the ability to share your video with others via iChat. Apple calls this the iChat Theater. Here's how it works:

1. Start iChat.

2. Connect to the person you want to collaborate with. The person at the other end needs a camera-equipped system. This technique won't work if the other person has only audio.

3. Switch back to Final Cut.

4. Load the sequence you want to have that person view.

5. Select **View > iChat Theater > Start Sharing**. Starting playing your sequence. The other person will see and hear your sequence play on her system, while you will see and hear her. Your video will also appear in a small window in your iChat screen.

6. Navigate around your Timeline as normal; the other person will see everything that's displayed on your Canvas. However, she won't see you until you select **View > iChat Theater > Stop Sharing**.

● **EXTRA CREDIT**
To display the sequence timecode as part of the playback, select **View > iChat Theater > Show Timecode**.

● **NOTE**
iChat Theater is for the Mac only (PCs are not supported). The Mac must be running OS X 10.5 or later and have video cameras installed; however, only the system originating the video needs to have Final Cut Studio (3).

Green Is Not Just for Stoplights
What those green buttons can show you.

On the left side of the Timeline is a series of green buttons, which I'll call "green visibility lights." There is one light for each track. These buttons are enormously powerful, but quite shy—they rarely tell us how much power they have.

When a green light is lit, everything on that track is visible (or audible). When a green light is dark, everything on that track is invisible (or inaudible).

But the impact of these buttons is much deeper than this. These buttons control output and export. If the light is dark, *nothing* on that track will be seen, heard, rendered, output, or exported.

You can use these buttons in a variety of ways:

- To see a clip hidden below another clip
- To keep source audio files in the Timeline but only hear the final mix
- To switch between displaying, say, English title keys (on track 4) and Spanish title keys (on track 5)
- To display/hide clips that you move from one section of a sequence to another, as you figure out which clip you want to use

These visibility lights give you the power to control exactly what is displayed and what is hidden.

● NOTE

When you change the visibility of a track, you lose your render files. (Yes, Final Cut warns you.) This is because render files are associated with the sequence, not the clip, and since you're changing what is visible in the sequence, the render files need to change.

Visibility Lights and the Arrow Keys
Those green lights control more than audio and video.

Did you know that the visibility lights also have an effect on the behavior of the Up/Down arrow keys?

Normally, when the visibility lights are on, the video is visible, the audio is audible, and pressing the Up/Down arrow keys jumps to the next/previous edit point on every track.

However, when the visibility lights are off, the video on that track becomes invisible, the audio on that track becomes inaudible, and pressing the Up/Down arrow keys skips all edit points on the now-hidden track.

More Visibility Shortcuts
This keyboard shortcut quickly makes a clip invisible—or the opposite.

To quickly toggle clip visibility on and off, select the clip, or clips, you want to hide and press **Control+B**.

While you can hide an entire track using the green visibility lights, sometimes you only need to hide a clip or two. Also, this method means that you don't lose your render files for an entire track, but just the render files for the clips you're hiding, or revealing.

This is a handy trick for comparing cutaways, B-roll, or alternative shots by simply toggling their visibility.

- **EXTRA CREDIT**

  When you're done comparing clips, because they're all gathered on a single track, you can cut and paste the clips into another sequence labeled Unused Clips. That way, they'll be handy in case you want them for later versions.

The Secrets of the Right-Pointing Arrow
It's almost impossible to see... and equally impossible to live without.

A great deal of the look of the Timeline is controlled from an itty-bitty right-pointing arrow at the bottom of the Timeline. It is certainly not obvious, so look closely just to the right of the four-column track height bar chart.

Click the arrow and look at all the choices you have. Each of these is a toggle. Select, or deselect, each one and watch what happens.

● **NOTE**
Some of these options have their own keyboard shortcut, but most don't. Without knowing about this arrow, you couldn't access many of these features.

Displaying Audio or Video Clip Names
Discover another use for that little arrow.

Remember that small, right-pointing arrow I just mentioned? Well, here's why it's nice to know.

Starting with Final Cut Pro 6.0.2, you can now toggle the display of audio or video clip names in the Timeline. This is useful when you're trying to set audio levels or opacity keyframes and the clip name keeps getting in the way.

The only problem is that this toggle is darn near impossible to find.

At the bottom of the Timeline, just to the right of the small bar chart, is that tiny right-pointing arrow. Click it and check, or uncheck, the clip names you want to hide.

They can be turned back on by repeating this same process.

● **EXTRA CREDIT**
You can also use this pop-up menu to turn on, or off, the display of audio waveforms in the Timeline.

Display a Filmstrip of Images in the Timeline

One mouse click and your Timeline displays your clip as a filmstrip of images.

Normally, the default display of the Timeline is a thumbnail image of the In point, followed by a bar of solid color. Most of the time this is fine for editing.

But, every so often, it would be great to see more of the images contained in a clip. Showing them is easy but not intuitive. (Although by now, I suspect you know where to look.)

In the bottom of the Timeline is that small right-pointing arrow, just to the right of the bar chart that allows you to change the Timeline track height.

Click and hold the arrow until a pop-up menu appears. Select **Show Video Filmstrips** to display images of all your clips in the Timeline.

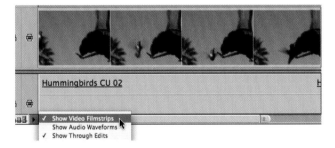

> **NOTE**
>
> Your Timeline images will look better the taller the track height. Also, the more you zoom into a clip, the more individual frames you'll see.

Displaying Source or Auxiliary Timecode
Here's a fast way to switch your display between timecode tracks.

Every QuickTime video clip can have up to three timecode tracks. These tracks are called Source, Aux 1, and Aux 2.

Most of the time, your video files will only have one timecode track. Sometimes, though, you may need to have the same video clip relate to two different timecodes—for instance, the timecode of the video recorded by the camera, and the timecode of an audio track playing off a separate device for a music video. This process of recording on two different devices—one for video and one for audio—is called double-system recording.

By default, only the source timecode is displayed in the Viewer or the Timeline. However, you can change this with a mouse click. Here's how:

Control-click the numbers inside the timecode box in the top-right corner of either the Viewer or Canvas. At the bottom of the pop-up menu you'll be able to select between all the timecode tracks available in that clip.

● NOTE

In order for this option to appear, the video clip must contain more than one timecode track. I say "video clip," because, except for Broadcast WAV audio files, audio files don't contain timecode. Chapter 3 shows how to add or change timecode.

Display Field Interlacing

By default, Final Cut Pro hides interlacing. Here's how to turn it on.

Interlacing is a fact of life for NTSC, PAL, and some HD formats. The problem is that Final Cut Pro keeps it hidden—which is fine until you have a flicker problem or need to export a freeze frame. At that point, it would be great to see what the interlacing looks like.

Interlacing was invented back in the mid-1930s when TV was developed. It solved problems with video camera imaging and analog broadcast transmission. But, as we move into all-digital video editing, it drives us completely nuts.

An interlaced image displays every other video scan line (2-4-6-8…), then overlays it with the remaining scan lines (1-3-5-7-9…). The first field is called the *even* (or *lower*) field, because it contains all the even lines. The second field is called the *odd* (or *upper*) field, because, as you've probably guessed, it contains all the odd-numbered lines. They are shot and displayed a fraction of a second apart.

It's that fraction of a second that causes the problem. If you have a rapidly moving object, this difference in time causes thin horizontal lines to radiate from all moving edges when you superimpose the earlier field on the later one.

To see interlacing, go to the rightmost of the three pop-up menus in the top center of the Viewer or Canvas and set the zoom percentage to **100%**.

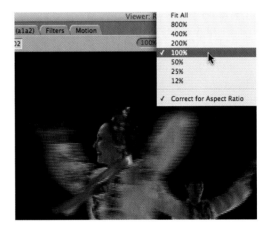

There's nothing inherently wrong about interlacing—it's a part of the video format. TV sets don't show it at all. However, when viewing video on a computer monitor, interlacing can be very distracting, which is why Final Cut hides it in the first place.

● **EXTRA CREDIT**

Don't remove interlacing during your video edit; doing so will remove half your video resolution. The best time to remove interlacing is when you are compressing your finished movie for the Web. (See Chapter 8.)

Duplicating Browser Clips
Four tips to faster copies!

Here are four quick and easy ways to make a copy of a clip or sequence in the Browser:

- Control-click your clip(s), or sequence(s), and select **Duplicate as New Master** from the context menu.
- Select the clips(s) you want to duplicate, then choose **Edit > Duplicate**.
- Select the clips(s) you want to duplicate, then press **Option+D**.
- Grab the clip in the Browser, drag it up on top of the Name column header, and let go.

Instant duplication!

● **EXTRA CREDIT**
You can also duplicate a clip by dragging it from the Browser of one project to the Browser of a second project.

Sorting Browser Columns
Ever wanted to reorganize the data in a Browser column?

The Final Cut Pro Browser is, at its core, a database. This means that sorting your data is easy—if you know where to click.

- To sort on any column, click the column name in the header of the column. This sorts everything in that column in ascending order. See the pointed triangle? That indicates the order of the sort.
- To sort in descending order, click the column header again.

● **NOTE**
Final Cut remembers the sort order of every Browser column when you quit the application. The next time you open it, everything will be sorted the same way.

Sorting Out Multiple Issues

You can sort on more than one column in the Browser—here's how.

The Browser is a database. This means we can search for stuff, examine stuff, and sort on stuff. (Stuff is, as you know, a technical term that means a "collection of somewhat related material that never contains exactly what you are looking for.")

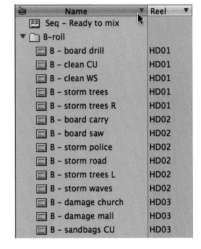

Maybe you want to group all your media by Reel ID, then sort it alphabetically by clip name. Or group all the good takes by day shot.

You can. As you just learned, to sort on a column you click the header of the column. But to sort on two columns, you need to know the secret handshake: the **Shift** key.

Click the first column you want to sort. It sorts alphabetically, with a small arrow on the right in the header indicating the direction of the sort. Then, hold the **Shift** key and click the second column header. Now you're sorting by two columns. Both columns now have arrows indicating the direction of the sort.

To change the sort in either column from ascending to descending, click the appropriate column header again. To cancel the sort, click any column header except one of the two columns you are sorting.

Here, for instance, I'm sorting first on **Reel ID** (it's highlighted with a down-pointing arrow), then by **File Name** (it also has an arrow).

NOTE

Final Cut Pro 7 allows sorting on at least three columns.

EXTRA CREDIT

To make it easier to sort on two widely separated columns, grab a column header and drag it to move the columns closer together.

A Faster Way to Move Columns
Here's a neat trick for moving columns in the Browser.

The Browser displays 37 columns. And, if you know where to look, there are another 30 columns hidden not too far away.

A column that I find useful, especially when capturing material, is the Reel ID. However, it's buried way out in the wilderness of the Browser.

Here's a fast way to move it, or any other column:

1. Scroll over to the Reel ID column.
2. Control-click the column header and select **Hide Column**.
3. Scroll to where you want that column to appear.
4. Control-click the column header that you want on the *right* of the moved column. (In our example, to put the Reel ID column to the left of the Duration column, we click the Duration column header.)
5. Select the name of the column you just hid from the pop-up menu; in our example, it's Reel ID.

Poof! The new column is instantly displayed to the *left* of the column header you just clicked.

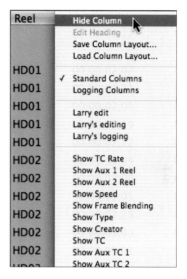

● **EXTRA CREDIT**

To display any one of the 30 hidden columns, Control-click any column header and select it from the pop-up menu. You can also use this menu to hide any column.

Customize Browser Columns
You can customize Browser columns—discover how here.

Final Cut Pro allows you to rename any Browser column heading that has the word *Comment* in the heading. Four of these (Master Comment 1, Master Comment 2, Comment A, and Comment B) are easy to find—just scroll to the right in the Browser.

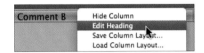

You can also display two more hidden comment fields (Master Comment 3 and Master Comment 4) by Control-clicking any column heading *except* the Name column.

To rename any of these column headers, Control-click the header and select **Edit Column Name**. Double-click the highlighted column name to select it, type the new name, and press **Enter** to lock it in.

● **EXTRA CREDIT**
Should you press **Enter** on the keypad or **Return** on the keyboard? I've discovered that for locking in the contents of a field, using the **Enter** key works more reliably, as the two keys are not always programmed the same. The good news is that both laptops and standard keyboards contain an Enter key. I recommend using it.

Searching Browser Columns
The best thing about a database is searchability. The Browser has it, too!

Looking for something in an overcrowded Browser?

To find the information you want:

1 Select the Browser (or press **Command+4**).

2. Choose **Edit > Find** (or press **Command+F**).

3. Select the column(s) you want to search. (**Any Column** is always a good place to start.)

4. Type the keyword or phrase you want to locate and click **Find All**.

Final Cut Pro displays all the clips that match your criteria in a separate Find Results window.

● **NOTE**
If you've renamed a Comment column header in the Browser, as we did in the previous Power Skill, you need to search using the column's original name. Final Cut Pro does not display the new column name in the column pop-up list.

Searching Effects
The Browser is searchable—and so is the Effects tab.

While we're on the subject of finding stuff…
did you know the Effects tab in the Browser is
searchable as well?

Select the **Effects** tab, then choose **Edit > Find**.

Type in a few letters of whatever you're
looking for.

The results will appear in a separate Find Results
dialog window once you click **Find All**.

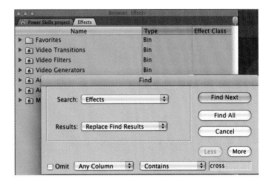

Viewing Thumbnails in the Browser
Not just view, but scrub them, too… and without going into Light Table view.

By default, thumbnails are hidden in the Browser. But like
many features inside Final Cut Pro, they're lurking just
beneath the surface.

Here's how to get them to stop hiding:

1. Control-click any column header except the Name column.
2. From the pop-up menu, select **Show Thumbnails**.

● **EXTRA CREDIT**

Using the Arrow tool, click and drag any thumbnail in the Browser to scrub
through it.

● **EXTRA CREDIT**

To change the image displayed in the thumbnail, called the Poster Frame, use
the Arrow tool to drag to the frame you want to use, press the Control key,
and let go of the mouse. Poof! Instant new poster frame.

● **NOTE**

Thumbnails in the Timeline are always
based on the In point. Poster frames are
only displayed in the Browser.

Display Images Instead of Names in the Browser

Lurking beneath the lists of files in the Browser is a digital light table just waiting to glow.

Most of the time, the alphanumeric name listings of files in the Browser work great. But when you're cutting action or images, it would be great to see the pictures all laid out nice and pretty.

You can.

In the Browser, Control-click in the gray area of the **Name** column and select the size icon you want to view. I generally choose **Large Icons**. (There's a cool keyboard shortcut that does this. Select the Browser and type **Shift+H** over and over and watch what happens!)

Grab the "thumb" in the lower-right corner of the Browser window and drag the entire window much bigger. All your clips are displayed as images rather than filenames. This is called the "Light Table" view.

Select the **Hand** tool (there's no keyboard shortcut when you're working in the Browser) from the Tool palette and drag a thumbnail to scrub an image.

Double-click an image to load it into the Viewer to set an In or Out point.

You'll find this method of working can help a lot when you're selecting images based on what the images look like, as opposed to how the clips are named.

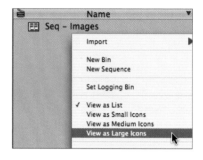

● **EXTRA CREDIT**

You can change the poster frame (the initial image) of a clip by dragging the image with the Hand tool. When you find the frame you want, press the **Control** key and let go of the mouse.

Fancy Light Table Tricks
You can edit a group of clips directly from the light table.

While we're looking at our clips in Light Table mode in the Browser, there's another interesting trick I can show you: how to edit a group of clips directly from the Browser into the Timeline.

First, drag the Browser so it's big enough to work in. Then, as you're looking at your clips, drag them into a rough tic-tac-toe shape. Put the starting clip at the top left, then build out the first row in the order you want your clips to edit to the Timeline.

If you need to set an In or Out point, double-click a clip to load it into the Viewer and mark the clip as you would normally.

When you're satisfied with the order and durations of your clips, drag a rectangle around them to select the entire group. Then, either drag the entire group to the Timeline, or—and this is my preference—drag the group to the Canvas and drop it on the red Overwrite overlay button. Either technique instantly edits all your clips into the Timeline. Dragging to the Overwrite button has the added benefit of editing the clips so that the group starts at the position of the playhead in the Timeline.

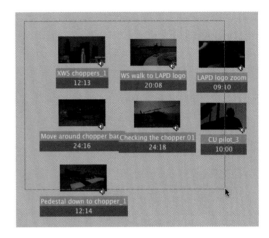

● NOTE

The order of the clips is determined by their position. The highest clip to the left is first, followed by the first row. If a clip in the middle of a row is higher than those to the left of it, Final Cut Pro considers it a row unto itself and edits it before others in the row. For this reason, consider setting your clips so their position runs slightly downhill to the right for each row.

More Browser Fun

New in Final Cut Pro 7, we can color-code, move, and close Browser bins and tabs.

We've been able to color-code clips using labels for a while. Now we can do the same with bins. In the Browser, Control-click the icon for a bin and select the label and color for the bin.

Double-click a bin to open it into a separate window. Drag the tab for a bin up next to other tabs at the top of the Browser. This docks it at the top of the Browser. Yes, we've been able to move bins for a while too—but putting them back is new. What is also new is that the color of the bin is displayed in the tab at the top of the Browser.

Control-click the name of any bin docked at the top of the Browser, and select **Close Bin** to close the bin and put it back into the main Browser window.

Control-click the name of any bin docked at the top of the Browser, and select **Close All Bins** to close all open bins and return all of them to the main Browser window.

● **NOTE**

The Project tab now has its own unique icon so you can tell the difference between a project and a bin.

● **NOTE**

Final Cut Pro 7 also displays color tabs in the Viewer if you've applied a label to a clip. Also in Final Cut Pro 7, if you apply a label to a sequence in the Browser, the color of the sequence tab in the Timeline reflects the color of the label you applied. (I only mention these here because I'm not talking about labels anywhere else in the book.)

● **EXTRA CREDIT**

No, we can't change the color. We've been working with these same tacky colors for some time now. You can change label names, however, by choosing **Final Cut Pro > User Preferences > Labels**.

Browser Keyboard Shortcuts
In the latest version, Apple added new keyboard shortcuts for bins.

To create a new bin, press **Command+B**.

To open a bin in a new Browser tab, select the bin and press **Option+Enter** (not Return).

To move between tabs, press **Shift+Command+[** (left square bracket) to move left one tab or **Shift+Command+]** (right square bracket) to move right one tab.

To close a selected tab, press **Control+W**.

● **EXTRA CREDIT**
To jump to a clip in a selected bin, just type the first few letters of its filename.

Hidden Tricks with Tabs
Learn the deepest secrets of tabs.

When in doubt, grab something and drag it. As an interface rule, it works, but how *déclassé* (um, "low class").

We need something cooler. So, here's a small flock of stuff to try:

- You can move a tab, like the Motion tab or Frame Viewer, by dragging it into another window.
- You can reorder tabs in the Timeline, or other window, by dragging them to a new position in the same window.
- You can enlarge a tab by selecting it and clicking the **Expand Window** button in the top-left corner of any window (see the screen shot).
- You can jump between tabs in the active window by pressing **Shift+Command+[** or **Shift+Command+]**.
- You can drag a window by pulling on its title bar or by pressing **Option+Command** and dragging the window from anywhere inside it.
- You can close a tab by Control-clicking it and selecting **Close Tab**.

Jumping Between Tabs
Here's a great keyboard shortcut that isn't just for the Browser.

This keyboard shortcut jumps between tabs in *any* open window, not just the Browser.

Press **Shift+Command+[** (left square bracket) to move to the tab on the left.

or

Press **Shift+Command+]** (right square bracket) to move to the tab on the right.

● **NOTE**

While it's cool to quickly move between tabs, when it comes to the Timeline, the more sequences you have open at once, the slower your system will run. Keep open sequences to a minimum.

Riddle Me a Riddle
When can you select something with *no* risk of moving it?

Answer: When you use the correct tool.

In this case, the **Group Selection** tool does exactly that.

It selects just like the Arrow selection tool. However, using the Arrow tool you can select *and* move things. With the Group Selection tool, you can select but *not* move things.

Try it and see.

● **EXTRA CREDIT**

The Group Selection tool's keyboard shortcut is **GG**.

Selecting Multiple Clips
The number one interface rule for Final Cut Pro is "Select Something, then Do Something to It."

While this may not be as deep as "I think, therefore I am" this interface rule will stand you in good stead as you figure out how to do something.

For instance, you can click, **Shift-click**, and **Command-click** clips to select them. This is cool, but there is a whole raft of little-used track selection tools that can make this process even easier.

The five track selection tools allow you to select multiple clips on one or more tracks:

When you use the first tool (press **T**), it selects all clips in a single track to the *right* of where you click.

The second tool (press **TT**) selects all clips in a single track to the *left* of where you click.

The third tool (press **TTT**) selects all clips in a single track, regardless of where you click.

The fourth tool (press **TTTT**) selects all clips in all tracks to the *right* of where you click.

The fifth tool (press **TTTTT**) selects all clips in all tracks to the *left* of where you click.

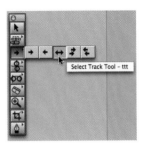

EXTRA CREDIT

Holding the Shift key when clicking switches a tool between selecting a single track and selecting multiple tracks.

NOTE

These tools select entire clips. So, if a clip extends into the range selected by the tool, the entire clip is selected.

Selecting an Edit Point
Wouldn't it be great if we had a tool that just selected edit points? We do!

And it's called the **Edit Selection** tool (press **G** to access it).

Grab this tool and drag a rectangle around the edit points you want to select. As you do, only the edit points, and not the clips, are selected.

Here's an added bonus: As soon as you select your edit points, the Trim Edit window opens, allowing you to quickly trim your clips.

● **EXTRA CREDIT**

Final Cut allows you to select only one edit point per track. For this reason, this tool is best used when you have multiple tracks with clips. Otherwise, just click an edit point with the Selection (Arrow) tool to select it.

Using Range Selection
Selecting a portion of a clip is easy—if you know where to click.

Sometimes, you need to select just a portion of a clip—say, to apply a filter to one part of a clip—without chopping the clip into multiple pieces.

You can do so using the Range Selection tool (press **GGG** to access it). Use this tool to drag across a portion of a clip to select a range within a clip. You can then delete a portion of the clip, or apply a filter to just that portion of the clip.

● **EXTRA CREDIT**

You can have an unlimited number of ranges in each clip, each with its own filter applied. To create multiple ranges, drag to select a portion of a clip, apply a filter, and then select another range and apply another filter.

Get Moving with Timecode

Timecode offsets get things to move quickly with precision. Here's how.

Here's a technique I use all the time to move things by a precise amount.

On the keypad, press **+** (plus) or **–** (minus), followed by a number, and then press the **Enter** key. Here's what happens:

- If nothing is selected, the playhead moves by the amount you entered.
- If a clip is selected, the clip moves, provided it isn't blocked by another clip.
- If an edit point is selected, the edit point moves, provided the clips on both sides of it have sufficient handles for the movement.

The *direction* in which something moves depends on the sign. *Plus* moves to the right; *minus* moves to the left.

The *distance* something moves depends on the number you type in. If the number you enter is two digits or less, Final Cut Pro considers it to be frames. If the number is four digits or less, it's considered to be seconds and frames. If it's six digits or less, it's considered to be minutes, seconds, and frames. Punctuation is not necessary.

So, typing **–20** and pressing **Enter** with nothing selected moves the playhead 20 frames to the left. Typing **+1200** and pressing **Enter** with a clip selected moves the clip 12 seconds to the right, provided it isn't blocked by another clip. Typing **+6** and pressing **Enter** with an edit point selected moves the selected edit point six frames to the right.

I use this technique all the time for trimming and positioning effects, because it's both fast and accurate.

Locking Tracks

Have you ever wanted to lock a track to prevent accidental changes?

Final Cut Pro has little padlock icons you can use to lock tracks to prevent accidental changes.

These are not for security—there are no passwords. Rather, these are intended to prevent the "Oh-my-GOSH, I-can't-believe-I-just-deleted-that! My-life-is-over!" feeling.

To lock a track, simply click the padlock icon. To unlock a track, click it again.

Hold the **Option** key while clicking a lock and every track *except* the track you click will lock. Option-click again and all tracks unlock.

For the keyboard obsessed:

1. Press **F4**, followed by [a number] locks, or unlocks, that video track.

2. Press **F5**, followed by [a number] locks, or unlocks, that audio track.

3. **Shift+F4** locks, or unlocks, *all* video tracks.

4. **Shift+F5** locks, or unlocks, *all* audio tracks.

● **NOTE**

I generally don't use track locks because I don't want to run the risk of knocking audio and video out of sync. However, when editing to a music track, I lock the audio tracks to avoid accidentally shifting the audio.

Toggling Display Modes

Here's a quick way to toggle between display modes in either the Canvas or Viewer.

There are three display modes for both the Canvas and Viewer:

- Image
- Image+Wireframe
- Wireframe

Image displays the image, but allows no effects adjustment, such as scaling.

Image+Wireframe both displays the image and the wireframe; it's most often used when you want to create motion effects for a clip by adjusting the clip in the Canvas.

Wireframe displays your image as an object outline; the key benefit is that it always displays in real time, no matter how complex your effects.

● **EXTRA CREDIT**

You can select these modes from the pop-up menu at the top of each window, but it's faster to toggle between them by pressing *W*.

Scrolling the Timeline

You have two ways to scroll the Timeline during playback.

It would be great if Final Cut's Timeline would scroll as our sequence plays… but it doesn't. Will that stop us when we can share another Power Skill that solves this problem? Certainly not.

If you don't have a scroll-wheel mouse, select the Hand tool (press **H**) and drag the Timeline up, down, left, or right as the playhead is rolling along.

If you do have a scroll-wheel mouse, put the cursor anywhere in the Timeline. Press **Shift** and roll the scroll wheel on your mouse to scroll the Timeline wherever you want.

● **NOTE**

Both these shortcuts work whether the Timeline is playing or paused.

● **EXTRA CREDIT**

Put the cursor at the bottom of the Timeline, where the zoom slider is located. Scroll and watch what happens. Yep, when you are at the bottom of the Timeline you don't even need to press the Shift key to scroll horizontally.

● **NOTE**

If you have an Apple Mighty Mouse, rolling the scroll wheel left or right will scroll the Final Cut Timeline.

Scrubbing the Playhead

Here's a fast way to scroll the playhead in the Timeline, Viewer, or Canvas.

Normally we just let the playhead play. But sometimes it would be nice if we could scrub it manually. Well, yes, you can grab the playhead and drag it, but how much fun is that?

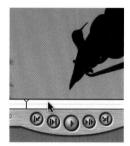

If you have a scroll-wheel mouse, here's something else you can do.

Put the Arrow tool in the timecode numbers at the top-left of the Timeline. Roll your scroll wheel, and shazaam! The playhead is scrubbing on its own.

The same technique works if you put the Arrow tool anywhere in either the Viewer or the Canvas. Roll the scroll wheel on your mouse and watch the playhead move on its own.

● **NOTE**
It could be argued that there are better ways to move the playhead. Perhaps. But you can always use this trick to impress people at parties.

Find the Missing Playhead

The playhead doesn't play hide-and-seek. Sometimes, it just gets lost.

Can't figure out where the playhead went?

Just click once on the small vertical purple line at the bottom of the Timeline to jump to the location of the playhead in the Timeline.

● **EXTRA CREDIT**
To scroll the Timeline horizontally, roll your scroll wheel in the area occupied by the purple line.

Scrubbing Timeline Thumbnails
I'm not sure why you'd do this, but it's a great party trick!

The thumbnails in the Timeline always display the image of the frame at the In point. However, you can scrub the thumbnail to see what's in the clip.

(Now, I realize some among you would point out that you can easily drag the playhead through the clip. But you'd be missing the larger point—this is a cool trick!)

Set the track height large enough that you can clearly see the Timeline thumbnails. Click the **Scrubber** tool (press **HH**) in the Tool palette. Then drag the hand inside the thumbnail image.

> ● **NOTE**
> Unlike with a Browser thumbnail, you can't change the still image the Timeline displays—it always displays the image of the frame at the In point.

Discover Project Properties
Projects have properties, too. Here's where to find and change them.

We normally think of projects in terms of their video format. You say, for instance, that you're "working on a RED project," or "finishing a P2 project."

However, projects have more properties than that. To see what your project properties look like, select **Edit > Project Properties**. The resulting properties dialog box is a great place to change Comment column header names, marker names, or marker visibility.

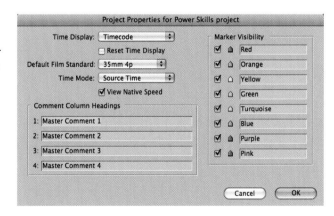

> ● **NOTE**
> Although you can change the Comment column header names in this window, you still need to enter the original column header name when using **Edit > Find**.

Markers Got Spiffed Up
Final Cut Pro 7 adds new capabilities to markers.

Final Cut Pro has two types of markers: Clip markers and Timeline markers. While their basic operation hasn't changed, the latest version of Final Cut Pro adds some welcome new features.

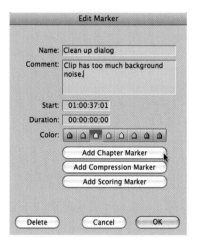

To create a marker, press **M**. If a clip is selected, the marker is created at the position of the playhead in the clip. If no clip is selected, the marker is placed on the Timeline at the position of the playhead.

With your playhead parked on a marker, press **M** again, and the **Edit Marker** dialog box opens. Here you can change the name of a marker, add a comment, and, for the first time, add a color to a marker. These colors show up in markers in both the Browser and the Timeline.

Here's the other cool thing. Timeline markers now have the option to reflect changes that ripple clips in the Timeline. If you delete a clip, or ripple an edit, that changes the duration of the Timeline, all downstream markers move up to remain in sync with the clips that just moved.

● **EXTRA CREDIT**

If you don't want markers to move as you make changes, click the new button to the left of the Link Selection button in the top-right corner of the Timeline. If this button (called Ripple Sequence Markers) is green, markers will shift position as clips move. If it's gray, markers will remain unchanged in the Timeline even if clips move.

● **EXTRA CREDIT**

If you want to create a marker and open the Edit Marker dialog box at the same time, press **Shift+Option+M**. You can use this during playback to quickly add a note to a clip or sequence without stopping.

Markers Can Be Moved!
Final Cut Pro 7 makes it easy to move markers.

Since the dawn of Final Cut Pro, editors have wanted to move markers manually. With the latest release we can—well, at least markers in the Timeline can be moved. In fact, Apple added a whole lot of marker tricks. Here's a quick list:

- To move a Timeline marker, press the **Command** key and drag the marker sideways.

- To delete a Timeline marker, press the **Command** key and drag the marker down into the Timeline.

- To open the Edit Marker dialog box, either double-click the marker while holding the **Command** key or place the playhead on the marker and press **M**.

- To add a marker and open the Edit Marker dialog box at the same time, press **Shift+Option+M**.

● **EXTRA CREDIT**

To open the Edit Marker dialog box for a Clip marker in the Browser, Control-click the marker icon or name and select **Edit** from the pop-up menu.

A Better Way to Move Between Markers
Using markers makes jumping around the Timeline extremely fast.

You probably recall that you can jump between markers using **Shift+M** (to jump to the next marker) and **Option+M** (to jump to the previous marker). These shortcuts work great if your Timeline is small.

But as the Timeline gets longer, or as it includes more markers, using keyboard shortcuts isn't as fast as we'd like. So, here's the secret: Control-click in the timecode bar at the top of the Timeline. A pop-up menu appears and your marker names are all listed at the bottom. Select the marker you want and the playhead instantly jumps to it.

This trick makes navigating even huge sequences a piece of cake.

● **EXTRA CREDIT**

Name your markers clearly. Then, when you Control-click on the timecode numbers at the top of the Timeline, a list of all your markers appears at the bottom of the pop-up menu. Good names make it easy to know to which marker you want to jump.

Reading Clip Markers
Here's a great way to read comments in Clip markers.

Thanks to Stephen Kanter for the following tip:

Here's the scenario: An editor puts markers on her clips with detailed notes. She then edits the clips and markers into a sequence. What's the best way to read the comments in the Clip markers?

Here's one way to do it:

1. Select the entire sequence by pressing **Command+A**.
2. Set Playhead Sync to **Open**.

3. Use the jump to the next/previous marker shortcuts (**Shift+M/Option+M**) to jump from marker to marker. The source clips will automatically open in the Viewer (i.e., Match Frame is always "on" in Open Sync mode), and you can read the overlays in the Viewer as you step through the sequence markers.

Very cool!

Using Markers to Log Footage
Here's another great use for markers.

The first thing to keep in mind is that all editors hate to log footage. The process is both time consuming and depressing. Anything that speeds this up is a good thing.

This tip was sent to me by Dave Isser. Dave provides a fast way to review and log footage after you've captured it: "Far and away my favorite thing is to use markers to log footage. The great thing about this system is that you can play clips continuously without having to pause them, and it really expedites your workflow.

"To get the best results, I watch clips in the Viewer and mark them with an **M**. Then, while the clip is still playing, double-click the name of the marker in the Browser, rename it to whatever description you want, and then click back into the Viewer, all without having to stop the continuously playing clip!"

NOTE

Earlier versions of Final Cut Pro sometimes had problems displaying more than 25 markers in a clip.

Deleting Multiple Clip Markers
Here's an easy way to delete a range of markers attached to Browser clips.

To delete all the markers in the Timeline, or in a selected clip, choose **Mark > Markers > Delete All**.

Unfortunately, since Final Cut Pro doesn't allow you to select markers, you can't delete a range of markers in the Timeline. But what if you want to delete some of a clip's markers without getting rid of them all?

In the last Power Skill, we loaded a clip into the Viewer to use markers to log the clip. When you load a clip in the Viewer and then add markers

to it, a small triangle appears next to the clip name in the Browser. Twirl this arrow down to see a list of all the markers in the clip.

In the Browser, select the markers you want to delete for each clip. Press the **Delete** key and watch all of the selected markers disappear.

> ● **NOTE**
> This trick doesn't work for Timeline markers or clips that have been edited to the Timeline.

Markers Have Default Colors
Track what markers mean using their default colors.

Not only can we add color to our markers, but some markers have default colors, which we can use to keep track of what markers mean:

- DVD Chapter markers are purple.
- Compression markers are blue.
- Audio scoring markers are orange.

Marker colors also show up as color backgrounds when markers are displayed in either the Viewer or Canvas.

> ● **EXTRA CREDIT**
> You can determine which markers appear in the Timeline by choosing **Edit > Project Properties**. In the Properties dialog box, you can change the marker name, or make all markers of one color invisible. You're not deleting markers; you're just hiding (or showing) them.

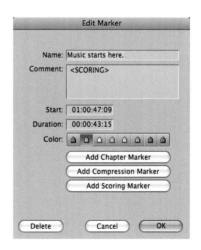

Using Markers in Multiclips
Here's another new marker feature in Final Cut Pro 7.

Another new use for markers is with multiclips.

Before creating a multiclip, you can review the individual clips you are about to edit. Add markers and marker comments. Assign colors to indicate something special about that marker.

Then, when you build the multiclip, the individual clip markers are retained in the multiclip. If a portion of a clip that contains the marker is edited into the final version in the Timeline, the marker appears as well.

You'll find this tip useful if you use your markers for making notes about a particular portion of a clip.

Option Means Opposite
It's Option key magic—all contained in one simple rule.

Final Cut Pro trainer Andrew Balis once described the Option key as the "opposite" key. Holding the Option key while doing something often (though not always) does just the opposite.

For example, Option-clicking an Audio Mute, Audio Solo, Visibility, or Auto-Select button turns on, or off, all the buttons, except the one you click.

Option-clicking with the Pen tool deletes a keyframe.

Option-clicking a linked clip selects just one side of the clip, either the audio or the video.

Option-clicking an edit point selects just the video or just the audio side of the edit.

Thinking of the Option key as an opposite key can open up a whole new way of speeding up your work.

Other Option Key Tricks
The Option key does duplication—watch!

The Option key offers the near-miraculous ability to duplicate just about anything.

For example, press the **Option** key and drag a clip. You are making a copy of the clip. Now it gets tricky.

If you release the mouse *before* you release the Option key, you will duplicate the clip and make an Insert edit, pushing everything downstream to make room for the duplicated clip. (The indicator is that the cursor points to the right.)

If you release the mouse *after* you release the Option key, you will duplicate the clip and make an Overwrite edit, replacing everything to make room for the duplicated clip. (The indicator is that the cursor points down.)

Hold **Shift+Option** and drag a clip up or down. This makes a copy of the clip and constrains the movement of the clip so that it only moves

vertically. This prevents a clip from getting out of sync. (This trick won't work if the audio and video of a clip are linked.) If more than one clip is selected, all selected clips are duplicated.

● **EXTRA CREDIT**

You can also use the Option key to move a clip. Start to drag a clip and don't release the mouse. Hold the Option key down and drag the clip so the left edge is where you want the clip to start. Release the mouse, *then* release the Option key. If you follow this order, your clip moves into its new position and all the clips between the old and new position shuffle to make room. When you do this correctly, the shape of the cursor turns into a curved, down-pointing arrow during the move.

The Fastest Way to Find a Keyboard Shortcut

The latest version of Final Cut Pro documentation doesn't provide a summary of keyboard shortcuts.

However, never fear... there's a much better way to see if a menu choice has a keyboard shortcut assigned to it.

Choose **Tools > Button List**. In the search box, type the first few letters of the menu choice.

Or just type a keyboard shortcut in the search box and see what it's linked to.

Or just type a letter to see all the different keyboard shortcuts assigned to that letter.

This is one place that I check regularly—it's sort of like reading a book for its plot—because this dialog box has an amazing cast of characters!

I Feel the Need—for Speed!
Eleven ways to make your Timeline play faster.

I was looking through the Button List menu a while back and discovered 11 keyboard shortcuts you may not know about that can make your Timeline play faster:

Control+F2: Play in reverse at 5x speed

Control+F3: Play in reverse at 4x speed

Control+F4: Play in reverse at 3x speed

Control+F5: Play in reverse at 2x speed

Control+F6: Play in reverse at 1x speed

Control+F7: Play forward at 1x speed

Control+F8: Play forward at 2x speed

Control+F9: Play forward at 3x speed

Control+F10: Play forward at 4x speed

Control+F11: Play forward at 5x speed

Control+F12: Play forward at 6x speed

Some of these are similar to pressing **J** multiple times to go in reverse, or **L** multiple times to go forward.

Don't you love discovering new things!

● **EXTRA CREDIT**

Here are two more keyboard shortcuts that are relevant: Press **K+L** to move forward at one-third speed. Press **K+J** to move in reverse at one-third speed.

● **EXTRA CREDIT**

Some of these keyboard shortcuts may be blocked by the OS or other software. To see a complete list of keyboard shortcuts for playback, select **Tools > Button List** and enter **Play** in the search box.

Create a Custom Keyboard Shortcut
Customize your own keyboard shortcuts.

Just as you can customize buttons, you can create customized keyboard shortcuts and save them to disk.

The process is simple:

1. Select **Tools > Keyboard Layout > Customize**.

2. Click the lock in the lower-left corner to unlock it.

3. In the search box in the top right, enter a portion of the menu text you want to search for. (Use lowercase to prevent confusion during the search.)

4. Click a tab at the top that corresponds to the modifier key you want to press when invoking the shortcut—for example, **Control**.

5. Drag the icon from the search list to the key you want to associate with that shortcut. In the figure, I'm dragging the Two-up window menu command into the **Control+Shift** tab

and onto the letter **U**. This creates a new keyboard shortcut to switch my window layout to a larger Canvas and Viewer using **Control+Shift+U**.

6. To save your newly revised keyboard shortcuts, choose **Tools > Keyboard Layout > Save**.

● **EXTRA CREDIT**

There is no limit to the number of keyboard shortcuts you can create. You can even save different collections into different files and switch between them using **Tools > Keyboard Layout** and picking from the list at the bottom of the menu.

● **NOTE**

Saved keyboard layouts are portable. As long as you store them in the same folder and location on each computer, you can easily transfer layouts.

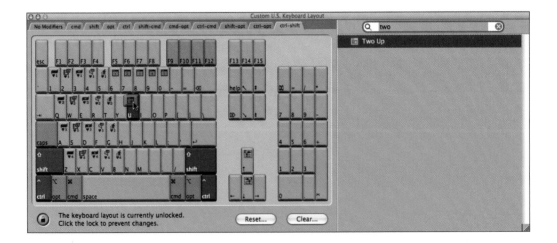

"A"—An Amazing Authority
One letter—eight keyboard shortcuts!

Here are some of the nifty keyboard shortcuts using the letter A:

Command+A: Selects everything in the active window.

Shift+Command+A: Deselects everything in the active window.

Shift+A: Sets In and Out points for whatever clip, or range of clips, is selected.

Option+A: Selects whatever clip, or range of clips, is marked by an In and Out point.

Control+A: Sets In and Out points between two markers containing the playhead.

● **EXTRA CREDIT**
And, pressing the letter **A**, all by itself, selects the Arrow (Selection) tool.

Wonderful, Wacky, W
Wonder What Wonders W Works?

The letter W is very talented, depending on what you need done. I use almost all of these daily.

Select either the Canvas or the Viewer and press **W**. Each time you press W, the selected window will change its display from **Image Only**, to **Image + Wireframe**, to **Wireframe Only**.

Control+W closes the selected tab in the active window.

Command+W closes the selected window.

Option+W toggles clip overlays in the Timeline (the red rubber bands and black opacity lines).

Control+Option+W toggles overlays on or off in the Canvas and Viewer.

Option+Command+W toggles audio waveforms on and off in the Timeline.

Shift+W toggles color channels in the Canvas or Viewer (RGB, Alpha, or Alpha+RGB).

Control+Shift+W applies the second favorite video filter.

There are many useful keyboard shortcuts in Final Cut, but none that revolve so closely around a single letter—W.

Wow!

How to Remove a Button
...in a massive puff of smoke!

Removing a button from a menu or window is easy. Just grab the button and drag it out of the button bar.

Poof! It's gone.

● **NOTE**
OK. I confess. Whenever I demo this to my classes, I always make the sound of an explosion. It helps get the point across. Really.

Creating a Custom Button
Every window can have its own buttons.

Just as you can customize the keyboard, you can also customize buttons. You can create individual buttons or build them into a complete button list that can be stored and reused.

Buttons can only be used to replicate menu items. You can't assign clips to buttons or create AppleScripts. Buttons in Final Cut don't allow you to create programmable sequences, like Photoshop Actions.

To create a button, choose **Tools > Button List** (or press **Option+J**) and enter the menu text, or keyboard shortcut, you want to turn into a button. It prevents confusing the search if you type in lowercase; so, for example, here I typed **fit**.

From the list of possible menu options, grab the icon for the one you want and drag it into the button bar in the top-right corner of the window you want it to appear.

● **EXTRA CREDIT**

To save the buttons you've created, select **Tools > Button Bar > Save** and give the current collection of buttons a name.

Reset/Remove All Buttons in a Button Bar
It's easy, if you know where to click.

Removing all the buttons from a single window can be done with a single click of the mouse:

1. Control-click any button.
2. From the pop-up menu, select either **Remove > All** or **Remove > Restore Default** (depends on the window you are in).

● **NOTE**

Only the Timeline button bar provides **All/Restore Default** as a choice. All other windows just display **Remove All**.

Additional Thoughts
Here's a collection of completely unrelated, but useful, things to know.

Each of these Power Skills is supposed to fill a single page of this book. But some are so simple and so short, they just can't be stretched to fill a page.

On the other hand, they're so useful, I can't, in good conscience, leave them out. So here they are—some of my favorite goodies.

- To play a portion of a sequence that requires rendering, without first rendering it, press **Option+P**.
- To load a clip from the Canvas into the Viewer, double-click it in the Canvas.
- To reset your windows to the default layout, press **Control+U**.
- To fit something into a window, press **Shift+Z**.
- To fit the selection into the Timeline, press **Shift+Option+Z**.
- To start Final Cut Pro without loading a project, hold the **Shift** key while Final Cut Pro starts up.
- To cancel any dialog box, press the **Esc** key.

CHAPTER 5

Editing

The whole reason you purchased Final Cut Pro in the first place was to learn how to edit. And the reason you purchased this book was to learn how to edit more easily, with better quality, while learning how to handle difficult situations.

Well, only you can decide where to put the In or the Out point, but once you've made that aesthetic decision, the Power Skills in this chapter will make the rest of your editing workflow fly. You're bound to find several skills here that will make a significant difference in your editing life.

Find It in the Timeline

Final Cut Pro can locate a specific frame in your sequence by using a clip from the Browser.

If you have a multitude of clips in your Timeline sequence and you're not sure if you used a particular shot or if you want to see where you placed it, this technique can help.

First, open the sequence you want to search into the Timeline. Next, open the Browser clip containing the frame you want to find into the Viewer. Position the Viewer playhead on the specific frame you want to locate in the Timeline and press **F**. If you used the shot in the active sequence, the playhead should jump right to it. (Think of this as a reverse match frame.)

This technique only works if it finds a match for that specific frame, but it can be a good time-saver nonetheless.

● **NOTE**
To find if you used a specific clip in your sequence, check out the Power Skill "Finding Unused Media," next.

Finding Unused Media

Here's a very fast way to find clips you haven't used in a sequence.

Editing documentaries often requires keeping track of hundreds of different files. However, all too often, it seems like you are constantly searching for some shot, *any* shot, that you haven't used yet to cover a jump cut or add necessary visual interest.

Here's a great trick that can help you find a shot you haven't used yet.

1. In the Browser, select the sequence you want to search.

2. Choose **Edit > Find** and choose **Unused Media** in the Find menu.

3. Make sure **in selected sequences** is checked, then click **Find All**.

All the clips you have not yet used in the selected sequence will appear in a separate Find Results window.

● **NOTE**
Final Cut considers a shot "used" even if you have only edited one frame from it into a sequence.

Two Fast Ways to Move a Clip Between Tracks
A keyboard shortcut or mouse click can move a clip between tracks.

First, here's the keyboard shortcut: to move a clip up or down between tracks, select the clip and hold down the **Option** key while also pressing the **Up** or **Down Arrow** key. Up moves the clip up a track and Down, not surprisingly, moves it down.

Here's the mouse move: press **Shift** and drag the clip you want to move. Shift constrains the clip so it only moves vertically and doesn't get out of sync.

● **EXTRA CREDIT**

If you only want to move the audio or video portion of a linked clip, press the Option key to select just the side of the clip you want, that is, the audio or the video. Then press the Shift key and drag the clip—or press Option+Up/Down Arrow—to move just the selected portion of the clip to the track you want.

Editing Is a Snap
However Snapping is set, it always seems to be wrong.
Here's how to change it.

When Snapping is on, whenever the playhead, a clip, or a tool gets within about 15 frames of an edit point, it snaps to the end of a clip.

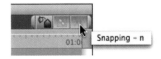

The keyboard shortcut for snapping is famous the world over as N—as in snnnnnnapping! (Steve Martin, of Ripple Training, may not have originated this line, but he is most famous for using it.)

You have several other ways to change snapping—one of which can bail you out of some tricky situations:

- Toggle the setting by choosing **View > Snapping**.
- Click the Snapping button in the top right of the Timeline.
- When dragging, press the **Option** key to toggle Snapping to the opposite of its current setting.

● **NOTE**

Using the menu, the letter N, or the Timeline button permanently alters snapping. Pressing the Option key only alters snapping until you release the mouse button; then snapping goes back to the way it was.

Faster Track Patching

Patching sets how audio and video routes from the Viewer to the Timeline. Here's how to control it.

The Patch panel on the left of the Timeline controls how the media in the Viewer edits into your sequence in the Timeline.

Specifically, it determines what tracks the video and audio go to. Since the Viewer holds only one track of video but up to 24 tracks of audio, this can be a complex thing to figure out. However, the Patch panel makes it easy.

For instance, grab the small, gray, **v1** patch on the left, which represents the video in the Viewer, and move it until it lines up with a patch on the right, which represents which Timeline track that video will edit to.

You can move the audio and video patches with the mouse, but a faster way is to use a keyboard shortcut. For example:

- Pressing **F6** followed by pressing the number **2,** moves the v1 video patch selector to connect to V2 of the Timeline.

- Pressing **F7** followed by a number moves the a1 patch.

- Pressing **F8** followed by a number moves the a2 patch.

This technique is easier to see than to explain. Press **F7**, then **3**, and watch how the a1 target track connects to A3.

Here are some more tricks:

- To disconnect the v1 patch, creating an audio-only edit, press **Shift+F6**.

- To disconnect the a1 patch, press **Shift+F7**.

- To disconnect the a2 patch, press **Shift+F8**.

● **EXTRA CREDIT**

Disconnecting both audio patches allows a video-only edit; disconnecting the video patch allows an audio-only edit.

Opening a Clip into the Viewer

Here are three quick ways to open a clip into the Viewer.

To open a clip into the Viewer:

- Select the clip and press **Return**, or **Enter.**

- Double-click a clip name or icon.

- Drag the clip in.

● **EXTRA CREDIT**

An interesting interface rule is "double-click a clip to load it into the Viewer." Whether you double-click a clip in the Browser, Timeline, or Canvas, in all three cases it appears in the Viewer.

A Fast Way to Reset the Patch Panel
One mouse click and the entire Patch panel resets.

The Patch panel controls which tracks a clip in the Viewer will edit to when you press the F10 key or click the red envelope in the lower left of the Canvas.

Personally, I use the Patch panel a lot and often need to reset it. I used to drag each patch back to where it belongs—until I learned this trick.

Simply Control-click anywhere in the left side of the Timeline and select **Reset Panel**.

Instant reset!

Opening a Sequence into the Viewer
There's the obvious way, and a double-extra-secret way, to load a sequence into the Viewer.

First, to load a sequence into the Viewer—either to review it or in preparation for editing it into the Timeline—simply drag it from the Browser into the Viewer.

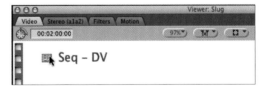

However, here's a much cooler way: To open a sequence from the Browser or Timeline into the Viewer, hold down the **Option** key and double-click the sequence.

● **NOTE**
This technique is great if you want to edit sections from one sequence into another sequence, or if you want to apply a filter to an entire sequence, then adjust the settings of the filter.

Deconstructing a Nest

Here's a fast way to move all the clips out of one sequence into another.

A nest is one sequence contained in another sequence. Nesting is the process of putting one sequence into another sequence. Most of the time, this works fine. But wouldn't it be great if you could instantly move the clips out of one sequence into another?

Well, you can—provided you take command of the situation.

1. Open the sequence to which you want to add the clips in the Timeline.

2. In the Browser, grab the sequence with the clips you want to add and drag it into the Timeline.

3. As soon as your cursor enters the Timeline window, and not until then, press the **Command** key.

Voilà! The sequence instantly turns into its individual clips, which you can add as a group in the Timeline.

NOTE

For those times when you want to keep the clips in the sequence nested, remember that Final Cut allows you to nest one sequence inside another inside another inside another... up to eight levels deep.

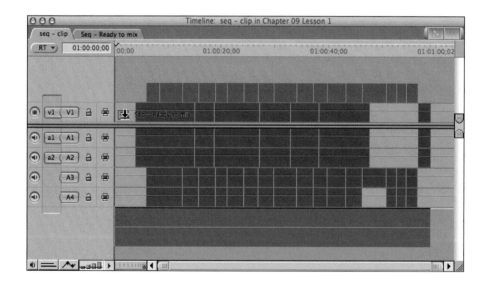

A Fast and a Faster Way to Edit
These two keyboard shortcuts *really* speed things up.

While you can drag clips from the Viewer to the Timeline, there are *much* faster ways to edit: one is a keyboard shortcut and one is a mouse click.

But first you need to know that Final Cut has two principal ways to edit: Overwrite and Insert. Once you have the In and Out points set for a clip in the Viewer:

- An *overwrite* edit replaces the footage in the Timeline that the clip from the Viewer lands on, starting at the position of the playhead. Overwrite edits never change the duration of the sequence (unless the clip is edited at the end of the sequence).

- An *insert* edit forces an edit point in the Timeline at the position of the playhead, inserting the Viewer clip, and pushing everything to the right of the edit downstream to make room for the clip. Insert edits always change the duration of the sequence.

- The keyboard shortcut for an overwrite edit is **F10**.

- The mouse click for an overwrite edit is the small red envelope in the lower left of the Canvas.

- The keyboard shortcut for an insert edit is **F9**.

- The mouse click for an insert edit is the small yellow envelope in the lower left of the Canvas.

● **EXTRA CREDIT**

There is another specialized edit: the Replace edit. The keyboard shortcut for this is **F11**, and the mouse click is the blue envelope in the lower left of the Canvas.

● **NOTE**

If your F-keys don't function the way you expect, read the Power Skills in Chapter 1 (pages 22 and 23) on how to reset the operating system.

What the Cursor Is Telling You
The cursor changes shape depending upon what it's editing.

When you drag a clip to the Timeline, the cursor has one of two shapes:

- A down-pointing arrow, which indicates you are about to do an overwrite edit; it's indicated by a solid brown clip.

- A right-pointing arrow, which indicates you are about to do an Insert edit; it's indicated by a hollow clip outline.

The shape of the cursor is determined by its position. If the cursor is positioned above the thin gray line about one-third of the way down from the top of a track, you'll do an Insert edit. If it's below that gray line, you'll do an Overwrite edit.

Toggling the Edit Point
An edit point has three sides—and we have a keyboard shortcut to select each of them.

To quickly toggle between selecting one of the three sides of an edit (that is, the In, the Out, or both), select the edit point with the Arrow tool and press **U** on your keyboard... do it again... and again.

The nice thing about this technique is that this works in both the Timeline and the Trim Edit window.

● **EXTRA CREDIT**

Select one side of the edit point, then press the **Up** or **Down Arrow** key and watch what happens. The selected edit point jumps to the previous (Up Arrow) or next (Down Arrow) edit point with the same portion of the edit point selected.

● **NOTE**

You can jump the playhead to the nearest edit point by pressing **V**. This selects the edit point as well.

Editing on the Fly
Introducing high-speed edits with one keystroke!

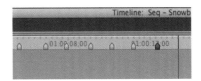

Did you know that you could add edits to a clip while playing the Timeline? This is perfect for cutting to the beat of the music in real time.

Here's the trick: press **Control+V** as the playhead moves across the clip. Final Cut adds markers as you go, and then creates the edits when you stop playback.

● **EXTRA CREDIT**

You can also use this technique when the playhead is stopped. Control+V is especially useful when you want to cut clips on multiple tracks all at the same point.

● **NOTE**

In Final Cut Pro 7 the markers are gray. In earlier versions, the markers are red.

● **EXTRA CREDIT**

You could also use this technique with the multitrack Razor Blade tool, but using Control+V doesn't require selecting a different tool. Plus, Control+V uses the position of the playhead to determine where the edits occur. The Razor Blade is more flexible in its positioning, but Control-V is faster.

Quick Cuts
Welcome to faster cuts with a keyboard shortcut.

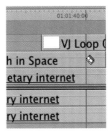

So, you're editing up a storm, slicing and dicing with the Razor Blade tool, when suddenly you come to a series of stacked clips.

The Razor Blade only cuts one linked clip at a time. You are stuck. Dead in the water. All that great mojo is fizzling away. You *could* drag your mouse all the way over to the Tool palette and select the multitrack Razor Blade tool—but you are moving way too fast for that.

Instead, press the **Shift** key—which instantly switches the Razor Blade into the multitrack Razor Blade—and just keep on rocking.

● **NOTE**

You could accomplish the same goal by pressing B twice, but that isn't nearly as cool.

A Faster Way to Do a Roll Trim
Roll trims are my bread and butter. Here's how to eat faster.

Select an edit point. Put your playhead where you want the selected edit point to move and press **E**. The selected edit point jumps to the position of the playhead—provided you have sufficient handles in your media.

This is essentially a Roll trim in real time.

Apple calls this an Extend edit. I call it fast and it is one of my favorite editing techniques.

> **NOTE**
> You can't jump an edit point over an existing clip.

> **EXTRA CREDIT**
> You can also do this in real time while playing the sequence. Just press **E** and the selected edit point jumps to the position of the playhead at the instant when you press the key—again, provided you have sufficient handles on each clip.

Rolling Edits on Multiple Tracks
Here's a fast way to roll edit points on multiple tracks.

Use this technique to adjust the timing of an edit point when using clips on multiple tracks:

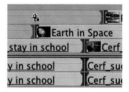

1. Toggle Snapping off (press **N**).
2. Make sure the Linked Selection button is on (green).
3. Select the Roll tool (press **R**).
4. Click the edit point you want to adjust on V1. This selects both the audio and video edit points.
5. Hold the **Command** key and click the edit point of the clip on V2. Since audio and video are linked, both audio and video edit points are also selected.
6. Drag the Roll tool to adjust the timing of all selected edit points.

Creating a Split Edit
Use this tip to have audio and video edit at different times.

A split edit is one where the audio and video of a clip edit at different times. But because the audio and video are linked (which maintains sync), selecting the video edit point also selects the audio edit point by default.

You can force Final Cut to select only the video or audio edit point by turning off Linked Selection. However, turning off the Linked Selection button when you want to move the edit points of a linked clip is an easy way to get your clips out of sync because this button turns off Sync Lock throughout the entire sequence until you turn it back on again. Very scary!

Instead, this tip makes the process much less risky:

NOTE

I can't stress enough how much easier, and safer, using the Option key is than turning off linking or Linked Selection. Using the Option key is temporary. As soon as you let go, linking resets to normal. The last thing you want is to forget you turned off linking, make a few changes, then discover that now your entire sequence is out of sync.

1. Select the Roll tool (press **R**).

2. Hold down the **Option** key.

3. Click the edit point (audio or video) you want to move.

4. Release the **Option** key and drag the edit with the Roll tool as necessary.

This is much safer and faster than using the Linked Selection button because it turns off linking only for as long as you press the Option key.

Creating Split Edits on Multiple Tracks
This is a very fast way to create split edits across multiple tracks.

Rolling just the audio or video is a trimming technique called "split edits" that allows you to change where the edit occurs in the picture without affecting the sound, or vice versa.

Avid editors often call these types of edit "L" or "J" edits. In an "L" edit, the video edits before the audio, with the two edit points forming the shape of an L. In a "J" edit, the video edits after the audio, forming the shape of a J.

To do the same thing for clips on multiple tracks:

1. Turn Snapping off (press **N**).

2. Select the Edit Selection tool (press **G**). This allows you to select edit points across multiple tracks.

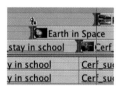

3. Hold the **Option** key and drag the Edit Selection tool around the edits you want to change. The Option key allows you to select just the audio or just the video of a linked clip.

4. Release the Option key after you've selected the edit points you want.

5. Select the Roll tool (press **R**).

6. Drag the Roll tool to adjust your edit points.

Ripple Delete
Yet another brilliant keyboard shortcut!

A ripple delete removes clips and pulls up all downstream clips on all tracks so that there are no gaps in the Timeline. Here's a neat shortcut for performing quick ripple deletes in Final Cut Pro:

1. Set In and Out points in the Timeline.

2. Press **Shift+X**, and Final Cut performs a ripple delete between the In and Out points.

● **EXTRA CREDIT**

I'm often asked how I edit. The answer is that I have one hand on the mouse and the other on the keyboard. That way, I can quickly use either a mouse shortcut or a keyboard shortcut, without spending a lot of time moving my hands.

● **NOTE**

Some editing systems—and Avid editors will know what I mean—require you to select clips on all downstream tracks before doing a ripple delete to keep things in sync. That's not necessary with Final Cut Pro, which handles trimming across multiple tracks automatically.

Multiple-Frame Trimming
This keyboard shortcut saves you hours when trimming clips.

When an edit point is selected, you can move the edit point one frame to the left, or right, using the comma, or period, keys.

But what if you are looking for a fast way to trim *multiple* frames at once from the end of a clip using the keyboard?

Select the In, Out, or both of the edit points you want to trim.

Press **Shift+period**. Ta-da! The selected edit point moves five frames to the right.

Shift+comma moves it five frames to the left.

You can do the same thing with **Shift+[** or **Shift+]**—but the period and comma may be easier for you to remember.

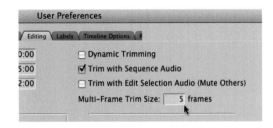

● **EXTRA CREDIT**
You can modify the number of frames trimmed when holding the Shift key; just choose **Final Cut Pro > User Preferences**, select the **Editing** tab, and adjust the **Multi-Frame Trim Size** option.

Sliding Clips
Sliding changes the location of a clip without changing its content or duration.

The Slide tool (shortcut: **SS**) allows you to change the location of a clip in the Timeline in relation to the clip before and after it, while keeping its content and duration unchanged. Thus, you are shortening the clip on one side and lengthening the clip on the other side of the clip you are sliding.

Sliding adjusts the Out point of the previous clip and the In point of the following clip.

You can slide a clip on the Timeline by selecting the Slide tool, clicking the clip you want to slide, and dragging it (or using the comma and period keys) to alter its location.

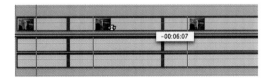

● **NOTE**
It helps to turn off Snapping (press **N**) when doing any trimming.

Creating an Asymmetric Trim

Here's an answer to a question that many Avid editors raise.

An asymmetric trim allows you to move the video edit point in one direction while the audio edit point(s) move in the opposite direction.

I get asked this question a lot because because Avid and Final Cut systems treat multilayer sync differently. So, in case you need to know, here's how to do it:

1. Select the Ripple tool (press **RR**).

2. **Option-click** one side of the video edit point (either the In or the Out).

3. **Command-click** the opposite side of the audio edit point (in other words, if you selected the video Out, Command-click the audio In).

4. **Command-click** any other edit points on all other tracks that you want to move.

5. Trim the selected edit point by dragging, pressing comma/period, or entering the number of seconds or frames you want to move.

This moves the selected edit points in opposite directions without losing sync.

● **NOTE**

During a standard trim, Final Cut Pro links all clips on all tracks. This means that if you ripple trim clips on V1 to pull up a clip, all downstream clips on *all* tracks will be pulled up automatically. In other words, Final Cut Pro is able to maintain sync automatically, without needing this specialized edit.

High-Speed Trimming
This may be the fastest way to trim.

Trimming is all about speed and accuracy. The reason we trim an edit point is to make the transition between the two clips flow as smoothly as possible. (To me, trimming is what separates a "home movie" from a professional edit.)

However, important as trimming is, we don't want to waste any time doing it. There's way too much work in any project to get bogged down trimming. So here's a high-speed trimming technique you can use on a daily basis:

1. Select the edit point.
2. Press **U** until the side of the edit point you want to trim is selected—In, Out, or both.
3. On the keypad, press the plus sign (**+**) followed by the number of frames, or seconds and frames, you want to trim; then press **Enter**.
4. The selected edit point will move to the right the number of frames you just entered.

To move to the left, press the minus sign (**–**) followed by the number of frames you want to trim.

I use this technique constantly because it is blindingly fast.

● **NOTE**
You don't need to add punctuation. If you enter one or two digits, Final Cut treats them as frames (i.e., 45 = 45 frames). If you enter three or four digits, Final Cut Pro calculates them as seconds and frames (i.e., 1234 = 12 seconds, 34 frames). Final Cut Pro does all the necessary math.

● **EXTRA CREDIT**
If you don't have a numeric keypad on your laptop, press **Shift+=** to move right, while you only need to press the minus sign (–) to move left on your regular keyboard.

Real-Time Trimming
The Trim Edit window provides real-time trimming—once you turn it on.

The Trim Edit window generates passionate responses from editors—both positive and negative. For those who edit audio, it's not particularly helpful. For those who edit action and movement, it can be invaluable.

One of the secret tips that makes this window so useful is that it can trim your edit points in real time—while you are playing your clips. Here's how:

1. Double-click an edit point to open the Trim Edit window.

2. At the bottom center of the window is a hard-to-see, gray **Dynamic** check box. When this option is selected, the Trim Edit window becomes real time.

3. To perform a trim, click the image for the clip you want to trim. The green bar indicates which clip is selected for trimming. Thus, to trim the Out point, click the left image; to trim the In point, click the right image. To do a Roll trim, click the vertical bar between the images.

4. Position the playhead before the point you want to trim.

5. Press **L** to play the clip.

6. When you reach the point you want to trim to, press **K**. This resets the selected edit point.

7. To preview your edit, press the **spacebar**.

> **NOTE**
> All trims made in the Trim Edit window are instantly passed to the Timeline and all clips are updated.

> **NOTE**
> Dynamic trimming remains on, even after you close the window, until you change its setting again.

Trim Edit Window Shortcuts
Here are six tricks to make trimming even faster.

The Trim Edit window is designed to provide a fast way to trim clips while you're watching them.

- To open the Trim Edit window, double-click any edit point.
- To select a Ripple trim, click in either the left or right window. The window that has a green bar over it is the clip that will be trimmed.
- To select a Roll trim, click the vertical gray bar between the two images. Roll trims are indicated by green bars over both windows.
- To set the In or Out point on the fly, press the **I** or **O** key while in Play mode. You can also set the In or Out point on the fly by clicking the **Mark In** or **Mark Out** button.
- Press **U** to toggle between selecting the In, the Out, or both points.
- In a hurry to know the duration of a clip? Look in the top-left corner of each clip.

● **EXTRA CREDIT**
You can also access the Trim Edit window by selecting an edit point and pressing **Command+7**.

● **NOTE**
To close the Trim Edit window, click anywhere outside it.

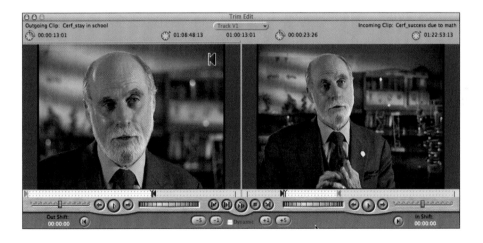

Using the Range Selection Tool
Here's a fast way to select only a portion of a clip without adding an edit point.

Wouldn't it be great to apply a filter to only a portion of a clip—without having to cut the clip into a million pieces first?

Well, you can—using the Range Selection tool (keyboard shortcut: **GGG**).

Using this tool, drag across a portion of a clip. Wherever you drag will be selected.

Now you can delete just this portion of the clip, copy and paste this part of the clip elsewhere, or apply a filter to the selected range. Whatever action you choose will only apply to the selected portion of the clip!

● **NOTE**
While you can select only one range at a time, your range can extend across multiple clips, or you can select the same clip multiple times to create multiple ranges within the same clip.

Getting Clips Back in Sync
First, you swear. Then, with one mouse click, you smile!

If you accidentally move a clip out of sync, don't worry! Here's a quick way to correct this.

Final Cut uses red "out of sync" flags to mark a clip that has been moved out of sync. To get an out-of-sync clip back into sync, Control-click the red flag of the clip you want to move and select **Move into Sync**.

If you don't want to move the clip but you want to get rid of the red flag, select the clip and choose **Modify > Mark In Sync**. Final Cut Pro now treats the new position of the clip as if it was in sync.

● **NOTE**
In some versions of Final Cut Pro, in order to see the red flag, **Show Video Clip Names** must be turned on (it's on by default).

● **EXTRA CREDIT**
If you clicked the video side of the clip but want to move the other side of the synced clip (for example, the audio), select **Move Others into Sync**. If you want the position of the video clip to stay put but adjust the contents so the video and audio are back in sync, select **Slip into Sync**. This option slips the video so the position of the clip doesn't change but the content moves so that it syncs with the audio.

● **NOTE**
You can generally avoid out-of-sync problems by never turning off **Modify > Link Selection**.

Setting Clip Durations
Here are five fast ways to change the duration of a clip.

Final Cut Pro uses two words to describe the length of a clip: length and duration.

Length is the total running time of the source clip stored on your hard disk. *Duration* is the running time between the In and Out points of a clip. Length can't be adjusted; Duration is adjusted constantly.

Here are several ways to adjust the Duration setting of a clip:

- Select the clip and press **Control+D**. This opens the Duration dialog box, where you can enter the new duration for a clip. When you adjust the duration, you are changing the location of the Out point.

- Control (or right)-click a clip in the Timeline and select **Duration** from the pop-up menu.

- Select the clip and choose **Modify > Duration**.

- For a clip in the Viewer, select the Viewer window and press the **Tab** key. The Duration dialog box opens, where you can specify a new Duration setting.

- For a clip in the Browser, change the entry in the **Duration** column for that clip.

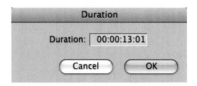

● **NOTE**

For clips in the Timeline, changing the Duration setting does a ripple edit, unless there's a clip on a track immediately above the altered clip. In that case, it shortens the clip but makes no other adjustments. Also, if the end of the altered clip has a transition attached to it, the duration of the clip can't be changed.

Changing Generated Clip Durations

All generated clips have a default 10-second duration. But you can change it.

By default, all generated video (bars, mattes, text—everything except slugs) has a 10-second duration. (Slugs, for some strange reason, have a 2-minute duration.)

To make generated video have a duration longer than 10 seconds, select the Viewer, press the **Tab** key (or click in the top-left timecode box), and enter the desired duration.

Pressing Tab opens the Duration dialog box in the top-left corner, where you can type whatever duration you choose.

● **EXTRA CREDIT**

In some versions of Final Cut Pro, you can change the duration by selecting **Final Cut Pro > User Preferences**, clicking the **Editing** tab, and adjusting the Still/Freeze Duration setting.

● **NOTE**

You can change the duration of a generated clip to any length—provided it has not been edited to the Timeline. Once a clip is placed in the Timeline, the maximum length is only 2 minutes.

Clearing Settings from a Group of Clips

Here's a fast way to reset clips in the Browser.

You can clear the settings for a group of selected clips in the Browser. Suppose you want to remove all the In points from a group of clips:

1. Select all the clips in the Browser that have In points you want to clear.

2. Control-click in the In column of the Browser and select **Clear In** at the bottom of the pop-up menu.

Poof. Gone.

You can reset the In, Out, Duration, Reel ID, as well as some other settings.

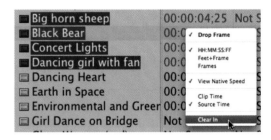

● **NOTE**

Clearing an In point means the clip will start at the beginning of the source clip stored on your hard disk. Clearing the Out point means the clip will end at the end of the source clip. Clearing the Duration setting means the clip runs the entire length of the source clip.

Deleting a Through Edit
You can eliminate those confusing red bowties in your Timeline.

When you use the Razor Blade (or **Control+V**) to cut a clip, you create an edit point that separates a clip into two pieces. This "through edit" is between two consecutive frames; thus there's no interruption to timecode, video, or audio continuity.

Normally, this is done to apply a filter or effect to one side of a clip but not the other. However, sometimes through edits occur because we cut a clip and forget to put it back. Through edits are indicated by red "bowties" at the edit points.

Well, unlike Humpty Dumpty, we can put this back together again.

To heal a through edit, do one of three things:

- Click the red bowtie to select it, and then press **Delete**.
- Control-click the red bowtie and select **Join Through Edit**.
- Control-click the red bowtie and select **Join All Through Edits** to make all your red bowties disappear.

NOTE

If there are effects applied to one side of a red bowtie and not the other, the settings of the clip on the left will be applied to the newly joined clip on the right.

The Fastest Way to Move a Clip
This mouse shortcut quickly moves a clip in the Timeline.

Need to quickly move a clip?

Shift-dragging allows you to move a clip vertically without allowing it to shift from side to side. If it's a linked clip, both the audio and video will change tracks.

If you just want to move a clip, another fast way to do so is to press **Option+Up/Down Arrow** key. As long as the audio and video aren't linked, this quickly moves a clip up or down a track.

EXTRA CREDIT

To select just the audio or video side of a linked clip, press the **Option** key. Once you have just one side of the clip selected, these shortcuts will work.

Duplicate Clips in the Timeline
Here are three ways to easily duplicate Timeline clips.

Say you have a clip on the Timeline that you want to duplicate.

Option #1: Select a clip(s), then **Option-drag** it. Final Cut Pro copies the clip and does an insert edit wherever you drag it.

Option #2: Select a clip(s), then **Option-drag** it, but *before* you release the mouse, let go of the Option key. Now, Final Cut Pro performs an overwrite edit.

Option #3: Select an audio or video clip(s) (but not both). Press **Shift+Option** and drag the clip. You'll make a copy of the selected clip, but constrain it so that it doesn't shift horizontally. This trick is very useful when you're creating duplicate clips for effects.

● **EXTRA CREDIT**
To select just the video or just the audio of a linked clip, press the **Option** key when selecting the clip.

Creating a Subclip
Subclips make it easy to divide a long clip into small chunks.

The basic capture rule of Final Cut Pro is to capture as short a clip as possible. Final Cut would prefer not to use long clips. But sometimes long clips are unavoidable. So, Final Cut provides a simple way to create a shorter clip from a longer clip; it's called a "subclip."

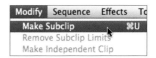

Subclips don't create any new media on your hard disk. Instead, they point to existing media, but instead of starting at the beginning of the file and going to the end, a subclip points to just a portion of it.

The nice thing about subclips is that they display with more detail in the Viewer, allow you to name the clip differently from the master clip that it was derived from, and, in general, help keep things more organized in your project.

● **NOTE**
You can also make subclips of sequences by loading the sequence into the Viewer and following the steps in the previous paragraph.

There are several ways to create subclips. One of the easiest is to load the master clip into the Viewer, set In and Out points that represent the portion of the clip you want to subclip, and then either select **Modify > Make Subclip** or press **Command+U**.

Copying and Pasting Between Tracks
The longest operational definition in Final Cut Pro...

Understanding how cutting, copying, and pasting work between tracks is the longest operational definition in Final Cut Pro, so brace yourself.

Definition: Final Cut Pro will always paste, as an overwrite edit, to the same track from which you cut or copied the clip unless, after you cut or copy the clip, you change the Auto-Select lights. If you change the Auto-Select lights, Final Cut Pro will paste the clip to the lowest numbered track whose Auto-Select light is dark.

So, if you want to cut a clip from V2 and paste it to V3:

1. Select the clip.
2. Choose **Edit > Cut** (press **Command+X**).
3. Move your playhead to the location where you want the soon-to-be-pasted clip to start.
4. On the left side of the Timeline, turn off (un-darken) the Auto-Select lights for tracks **V1** and **V2**.
5. When the **V3** Auto-Select light is dark, paste the clip. It will appear at the position of the playhead on V3.

● **EXTRA CREDIT**

A fast way to turn off all Auto-Select lights *except* the one you click is to hold **Option** down when clicking. To turn them all back on again, press the **Option** key and click the Auto-Select light that's dark.

● **NOTE**

Remember, you need to change the Auto-Select lights *after* you cut or copy the clip. Otherwise, it has no effect.

Copying and Pasting Clips from the Viewer
Where clips go depends on where they come from.

If you load a clip into the Viewer, select **Edit > Copy** (or press **Command+C**), then paste it into the Timeline (by pressing **Command+V**), the Patch panel on the left side of the Timeline controls which track the clip goes to.

● **NOTE**

If one of the patches is disconnected, that track won't paste into the Timeline. This is how to create a video-only, or audio-only, edit.

A Faster Way to Create Subclips
Markers make subclip magic.

Subclips can be useful ways to break a long capture file into individual scenes. But the process of setting In and Out points for each scene is… cumbersome. The reason you bought this book is that you are looking for faster ways, secret ways, to get your work done. Well, watch this:

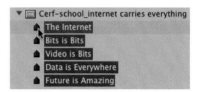

1. Load a long Browser clip into the Viewer. Place a marker (press **M**) at the start of every scene, or section, that you want to turn into a subclip.

2. Notice that as soon as you create a marker, a small triangle appears next to your clip in the Browser. Twirl that triangle down to reveal all the clip markers you just set.

3. Drag those markers into a bin. (To create a new bin, press **Command+B**.)

4. The instant the markers are dropped into a bin, they become subclips that use the same names you gave the markers.

● **EXTRA CREDIT**

You can always change the name of a Browser marker or subclip by clicking it; this is the same as changing the name of a clip.

Removing Subclip Limits
Reset a subclip to match the source media.

Since subclips don't really exist—they simply point to a portion of already existing source media on your hard disk—removing the limits of a subclip doesn't cause any media to be lost.

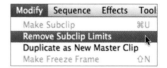

When you remove the limits of a subclip, the subclip reverts back to the same length and contents as the source clip on your hard disk.

To reset a subclip to match the source clip, open the subclip in the Viewer and select **Modify > Remove Subclip Limits**. The icon for the clip in the Browser switches from a subclip icon to a normal clip icon.

● **NOTE**

When you remove the limits on a subclip, any Timeline edits made with that subclip remain the same, but all clips affiliated with that subclip revert back to normal clips.

Many Ways to Match a Frame
Finding a match frame gets easier.

Sometimes you need to find the source clip for a clip in the Timeline. This is called finding the *match frame*. A match frame is a frame-accurate match between a clip in the Timeline and the source clip in the Browser.

There are several ways you can do this. Put your playhead in the Timeline on the clip you want to match. Then:

- Select **View > Match Frame > Master Clip** (or, much more easily, press **F**) to load the source clip from the Browser into the Viewer, matching the clip in the Viewer with the In point, Out point, and position of the playhead of the Timeline clip.

- Select **View > Match Frame > Source File** (or, also more easily, press **Option+Command+F**) to load the source clip from the Browser into the Viewer, matching the position of the Timeline playhead but not adding an In or Out point in the Viewer.

- Select **View > Reveal Master Clip** (or press **Shift+F**) to highlight the source clip in the Browser.

EXTRA CREDIT

The option **Option+Command+F** is especially useful when you want to do a replace edit based on the position of the playhead versus the In or the Out point.

Find Match Frames from a Subclip in the Timeline
Now you can match to the subclip or the source file.

Subclips are special kinds of clips. They don't really exist—they simply point to a portion of an existing clip.

So, when you need to find the match frame to a subclip, you have two choices: to find the *subclip* in the Browser, or to find the original *source clip* in the Browser. We've been able to do the first option for a while. The second option is brand new with Final Cut Pro 7.

To find the subclip in the Browser from a clip in the Timeline, put your Timeline playhead in the subclip you want to match and press **F**. The original subclip opens in the Viewer, with matching In and Out points and playhead position.

To find the source file for a subclip, put your Timeline playhead in the subclip, then press **Option+Command+F**. The original source clip opens in the Viewer and matches the position of the Timeline playhead.

New with Final Cut Pro 7 is the option to choose **View > Match Frame > Subclip Parent Clip**. This opens the parent clip (the source of the subclip) into the Viewer and matches the position of the playhead.

NOTE

Apple cautions that if you're working with a project created in an earlier version of Final Cut Pro, **View > Match Frame > Subclip Parent Clip** won't work.

Why Won't a Match Frame Match?
Because sometimes clips are independent…

When you edit a clip from the Viewer, or Browser, into the Timeline, the editing process creates a relationship between the master clip in the Browser and the edited clip in the Timeline. Apple calls this edited clip an *affiliate* clip, which is related to the Browser clip based on four criteria:

- Reel ID
- Filename
- Source timecode
- Auxiliary timecode

It's because of this relationship that match framing works. However, when you drag a clip directly into the Timeline, no master clip is created in the Browser. This means that while you can still find the source file on the hard disk that relates to the Timeline clip, match framing won't work.

● EXTRA CREDIT

To be sure to create a master clip, whenever you drag a clip into Final Cut Pro, drop it into the Browser first, then edit it to the Timeline.

● NOTE

Independent clips can also cause problems during media management and recapturing. Avoid creating independent clips. Also, try not to create more than one master clip (a clip in the Browser) that references the same source media file on your hard disk.

Opening Clips in Another Application
Here's a fast way to open clips in another program.

In the View menu is the option **Open Clip in Editor** (the shortcut is **Option+Return**). This menu choice also exists if you Control-click a clip. But what does it do?

Open Clip in Editor is a very fast way to open a clip in the application that created it—or somewhere else, if you prefer.

Assuming your preference files haven't been altered, this option opens:

- A QuickTime file in QuickTime
- A Motion project in Motion
- A LiveType project in LiveType (assuming you have LiveType installed on your system)
- A Soundtrack project in Soundtrack
- A Photoshop file in Photoshop

In other words, it opens the file in the application that created it.

But you can change this behavior. Choose **Final Cut Pro > System Settings,** then click the **External Editors** tab. Here, you can set what application opens a particular type of file. In this example, I'm using Photoshop CS4 to open both still and video files for image editing, and Soundtrack Pro for audio files. This option gives you one-click access for moving a file out of Final Cut Pro directly into another application.

NOTE

The Send option only works with Final Cut Studio applications. Open in Editor allows you to move a file to *any* application.

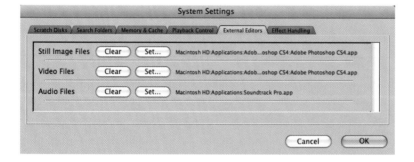

Find Clips in the Finder
Tracking down media files is really easy.

Recent versions of Final Cut Pro have made it increasingly easy to locate media files stored on your hard disk.

This is helpful when you stored—purely by accident, I'm sure—your media files in some really bizarre place. Realizing the error of your ways, you want to move them to a more logical location—except, you've forgotten where you first put those files.

Not to panic.

Select the clip you want to find—this works for clips in the Browser, Viewer, Timeline, or Canvas. The key is to first select the clip.

Next, choose **View > Reveal in Finder**. A Finder window opens in front of Final Cut Pro and your wayward file is highlighted.

● **NOTE**
If you move file locations in the Finder, you will break the links for those files stored in Final Cut. The first rule is: "Don't move files." If you must move files, relink them in Final Cut as soon as you get done moving them.

Reveal the Location of a Subclip's Source
Here's a surefire way to find a source clip in the Browser.

Match frames allow you to open a master clip in the Viewer so you can review it or edit it into the Timeline.

Sometimes, however, you just need to figure out where the source clip is located in the Browser. There are two ways you can easily do that. They all start with highlighting the clip you want to find in either the Viewer or the Timeline.

- Press **Shift+F** to reveal the location of the selected clip in the Browser. If it is in a bin, the bin will be opened and the clip name highlighted.

- Select **View > Reveal Subclip Parent Clip** to reveal the location in the Browser of the parent (source) clip from which a subclip was created.

Renaming Files in the Finder

Renaming a file is a sure route to disaster—unless you follow this procedure.

Apple designed Final Cut Pro project files to be renamed or moved to any location you want without breaking, but source files must not be renamed or moved once they are imported into Final Cut because that breaks the links to the files in Final Cut.

However, sometimes you just need to rename a file for completely valid reasons.

So, here's what you do to prevent a crisis: rename it in the Browser first. Then, select the Browser clip and choose **Modify > Rename > File to Match Clip**.

The "File" is the source file stored on your hard disk. The "Clip" is the name of the clip in the Browser. The huge benefit to this is that Final Cut Pro automatically updates its links when you rename the file so that nothing breaks.

Use this trick whenever you start renaming Browser clips so that the Browser and Finder clip names match.

● **EXTRA CREDIT**

If you've renamed a clip in the Finder and updated the link to the same clip in the Browser using **File > Reconnect Media**, choose **Modify > Rename > Clip to Match File** to change the Browser clip name to match the name of the source file in the Finder.

Comparing Two Clips or Sequences at the Same Time

Here's a great way to check two different clips or sequences in sync against each other.

Most of the time you don't want any connection between the Viewer and the Timeline.

But sometimes you do—for example, if you want to compare a low-resolution cut of a sequence with a high-resolution cut of the same sequence to be sure you have all the cuts in the right place.

Here's a neat way to accomplish this. The basic idea is to load one sequence (or clip) into the Timeline, then run it in sync with a second clip (or sequence) in the Viewer.

Start by opening one of the clips, or sequences, you want to compare into the Timeline. Put your playhead where you want the comparison to begin. Be precise, because this becomes your sync point.

Load the second clip, or sequence, you want to compare into the Viewer. Again, set your Viewer playhead precisely at the point you want to sync these two clips.

Open the center pop-up in either the Viewer or Canvas and set it to **Gang**. While the clips won't play in sync (for that, you'd need to create a multi-clip), you can view them both by dragging the playhead, using the Up/Down or Left/Right Arrow keys, or pressing **Option+P**.

● **NOTE**

You can use this to make sure the cuts between two versions match. The fastest way for you to compare is to use the Up/Down Arrow keys to jump both Viewer and Canvas to the same point. Also, if you use Option+P, remember that it won't play in real time but somewhat slower, which means you won't hear audio.

Finding and Eliminating Timeline Gaps

Gaps cause flashes of black—and ulcers. Here's how to get rid of them.

There are two kinds of gaps in Final Cut Pro:

- A *timeline* gap crosses all tracks in the Timeline.
- A *track* gap is a gap in one or more tracks, but other clips on other tracks span the gap. Generally, track gaps are only a concern for video and not audio.

This Power Skill talks about timeline gaps; the next skill covers track gaps.

Finding and eliminating gaps across all the tracks in the Timeline is easy to do:

1. Select **Mark > Next > Gap** (or press **Shift+G**) to move forward to the next gap, or select **Mark > Previous > Gap** (or press **Option+G**) to move back to the previous gap.
2. Click within the gap on any track to highlight it.
3. Press the big **Delete** key (above Return). No more gap!

● **NOTE**

If the Auto-Select button is turned off (it's hollow and light gray), any gaps in that track are ignored.

● **EXTRA CREDIT**

You can also delete gaps by Control-clicking a gap and selecting **Close Gap**, or by selecting **Sequence > Close Gap**.

Finding Track Gaps

Track gaps in video cause flashes of black—which can get you fired. Here's how to spot 'em.

A track gap in Final Cut occurs when a gap exists between clips on one track but has material over or under it on other tracks. What to do?

Generally, if a video clip is above a gap in a lower video track, you don't need to worry. The higher clip covers the gap in the lower track.

Also, track gaps in audio are normal, and unless you need continuous audio for that section, you have nothing to worry about.

But when a gap in a video track is covered by continuous audio, there's a problem. Worse, these gaps are often only a frame or two wide, which makes them difficult to spot.

● **EXTRA CREDIT**

To find gaps in only one track, Option-click the Auto-Select button for the track you want to search—most often this is the V1 track. Final Cut Pro will only search tracks whose Auto-Select buttons are dark.

So, to find track gaps, position the playhead at the beginning of the sequence.

Then choose **Mark > Next > Track Gap** and watch how Final Cut Pro jumps to the next gap in any track. To go back to a gap, select **Mark > Previous > Track Gap**.

To remove a track gap, see the next Power Skill.

Removing Track Gaps

Fixing a track gap can be tricky.

The previous Power Skill discussed how to find track gaps—gaps in a video track that are covered with audio.

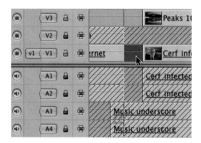

Once you've found a track gap, you can remove it in one of three ways:

- Stretch one of the clips on either side of the gap to fill the gap.
- Lock all tracks except the track with the gap, click the gap to select it, and press **Delete**.
- Pick the **Select Track Forward** tool (press **T**), click in the gap to select all clips in that track to the right of the gap, and drag the selected clips to close the gap.

Picking the best method depends on the amount of video in the clips before and after a gap and whether you need to worry about audio sync after the gap.

● **NOTE**

Because there are an almost unlimited number of ways to potentially fix a track gap, Final Cut does not provide an automated way to fix them.

A Faster Way to Preview an Edit

This keyboard shortcut makes it easy to preview an edit point.

Here's a fast way to preview anything at the position of the playhead. Press the backslash key (\) located immediately above the Return key.

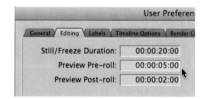

Watch how the playhead backs up a few seconds, plays through the current location of the playhead, stops for a few seconds, then resets the playhead to its original position.

This method of previewing is so quick, it's addictive.

● **EXTRA CREDIT**

You can change the amount of time the playhead backs up, or how far it plays past the edit point, by choosing **Final Cut Pro > User Preferences** and modifying options on the **Editing** tab.

Continuous Looping
Real-time review—over and over and over...

Not sure you like that edit? Want to see it a few times in a row?

To have Final Cut continuously loop playback in either the Viewer or Canvas, select **View > Loop Playback** (or press **Control+L**), set In and Out points on either side of the section you want to review in your Timeline (or Viewer), and press **Shift+/**.

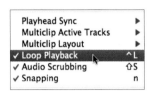

You are now stuck in a time loop from which there is no escape! (Actually there is: It's called the **spacebar**.) While this trick is most useful in the Timeline, it's nice to know this works in the Viewer as well.

● NOTE
The Trim Edit window also provides a real-time preview, but the Timeline is faster.

Copy Timecode from Window to Window
This is a quick trick that can save you lots of typing.

There are times when it's useful to match a timecode from one window to another—to match a duration, In point, or Out point, for example.

There are two solutions:

• Select the timecode by clicking the timecode icon next to the numbers; then copy (**Command+C**) the selected timecode from one Timecode data entry box and paste (**Command+V**) it to another Timecode data entry box.

or

• Make sure the timecode is not selected, then hold down the **Option** key and drag the timecode numbers from one Timecode data entry box to another.

Quick, easy, simple, and neat.

Continuously Loopy

Here's another way to view the same thing over and over in real time.

A special window is built into Final Cut Pro that allows you to view even the most complex effect in real time. It's called the QuickView window, and here's how it works.

Place your playhead in the middle of the sequence you want to review. (You can do this in the Viewer as well, but most of the time, you want to see an effect from the Timeline without waiting for it to render.)

Select **Tools > QuickView**. A window opens in front of the Viewer, with the playhead parked in the middle of the window.

The slider at the bottom allows you to adjust how many seconds of your sequence you want to view. The range is 2 to 10, centered on the current location of the playhead. For example, if you select **4** seconds, it backs up 2 seconds before the current location of the playhead, then plays for the next 4 seconds.

The first time the QuickView window plays, it builds a RAM preview, so it's slower than real time. After that, it continuously loops for the selected duration in real time.

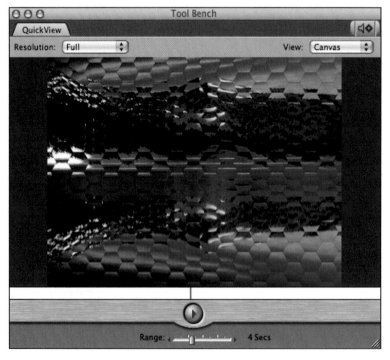

● EXTRA CREDIT

If you want a larger QuickView window, increase the size of the Viewer *before* you open QuickView, or drag the thumb in the lower-right corner of the QuickView window.

Get Things Moving
Here's a fast way to accurately move the playhead, clips, or edit points.

When in doubt, grab something and drag it. That admonition works great… when you're more concerned about speed than accuracy. But what about when you want to move something a precise amount?

Here's a great way to move something precisely:

- **Moving the playhead:** If nothing is selected in the Timeline, press **+** or **–** on the numeric keypad followed by a number, then press **Enter**. The playhead will move right (+) or left (-) based on the number you type in. If the number is one or two digits, it moves by frames. If the number consists of three or four digits, it moves by seconds and frames. If the number consists of five or six digits, it moves by minutes, seconds, and frames.

  So, type **+15**, and the playhead moves 15 frames to the right. Type **–35** and the playhead moves 35 frames to the left. Type **+1000** and the playhead moves 10 seconds to the right. Type **–13014** and the playhead moves 1 minute, 30 seconds, and 14 frames to the left.

- **Moving a clip:** Select a clip, then press **+** or **–** on the keypad followed by a number, then press **Enter**. The selected clip(s) moves left or right, based on the number you typed in, provided it's not blocked by another clip on the same track.

- **Moving an edit point:** Select an edit point, then press **+** or **–** on the keypad followed by a number, then press **Enter**. The selected edit point moves left or right, based on the number you typed in, provided there are sufficient handles for it to move that distance.

● **EXTRA CREDIT**

You don't need to use punctuation—you can just type the number. Final Cut Pro does the math for you—typing **99** is the same as typing **3:09** for 29.97 fps NTSC video.

● **NOTE**

If you don't have a numeric keypad, substitute minus (**–**) and **Shift+=** for the plus.

● **NOTE**

The **Enter** and **Return** keys are often programmed to do different things. For that reason, when you are accepting the contents of a data entry box, **Enter** always works reliably. **Return** sometimes adds a carriage return and leaves the dialog box open. For this reason, I recommend using the Enter key.

Changing Timecode
QuickTime files contain three timecode tracks.
Here's how to change them.

Timecode is at the heart of nonlinear editing. Sometimes timecode needs to be changed to properly sync separately recorded picture and sound, or to change a timecode setting chosen in the camera that does not work for you in postproduction.

A good example is a narrative film scene where the audio is recorded to one device and the video to another. And, as often happens, the audio and video timecodes are not the same. Often, you don't want to change the master timecode, but you do want to track both time-codes in the video clip.

To do this, select the clip with the timecode you want to change in the Browser, the Viewer, or the Timeline.

Select **Modify > Timecode**. Three timecode tracks are stored inside every QuickTime file: the primary and two auxiliary tracks.

In our example, I turned on the **Aux 1** timecode track by checking it. Then, I added a **Reel ID** to identify the source tape or folder and entered the timecode setting I wanted to use.

In the pop-up at the top, I indicated whether this timecode number should be set to the first frame of the clip or the current location of the playhead. A good reason for using the current location of the playhead is when you want to match timecode between audio and video ele-ments based on the location of a clapper slate.

● **EXTRA CREDIT**

To change the timecode that's displayed in the Viewer and used when editing that clip, load the clip into the Viewer, **Control-click** the top-right timecode box in the Viewer, and change it from **Source** to **Aux 1** or **Aux 2** at the bot-tom of the pop-up menu.

Multiclips and Markers
Keep these tips in mind when using markers with multiclips.

In Final Cut Pro, a multiclip combines a series of related shots into a special clip where you can see all the images at once when played in the Viewer.

Markers, as you know, are a great way to flag specific locations in a clip or the Timeline. With the release of Final Cut Pro 7, Apple changed the way multiclips and markers work:

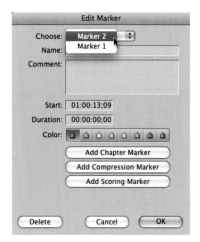

- If you load a source clip into the Viewer and apply markers before combining that clip into a multiclip, the Clip markers will be retained in the multiclip.

- When a multiclip is edited to the Timeline, any Clip markers in the active angle of the clip are displayed in the multiclip.

- You can apply Clip markers to a multiclip the same as a normal clip.

- Markers in a multiclip appear on the Timeline as Clip markers.

- Timeline markers for a sequence containing a multiclip behave exactly the same as markers for any other clip.

● **EXTRA CREDIT**

It's possible two markers may appear on the same frame. If that happens, open the Edit Marker dialog box for one the markers (a good way to do this is to put the playhead on a marker and press **M**), and select the marker you want to adjust from the **Choose** pop-up menu at the top of the window.

Adding Clips to Multiclips
Oops. You forgot to add an angle to a multiclip. Now what?

You have two choices in this situation, depending on whether you've edited the clip to the Timeline yet.

In either case, you start the same way: In the Browser, grab the clip you want to add and drag it into the multiclip you've loaded into the Viewer.

Then, *wait*! Don't let go. In a few seconds, a pop-up menu will appear. (There aren't a lot of these types of menus in Final Cut Pro, though DVD Studio Pro uses them frequently.)

If you drop the clip on **Insert New Angle**, the clip will be added to the multiclip in the Viewer, but not into any multiclips you've edited to the Timeline.

If, on the other hand, you drop the clip on **Insert New Angle Affiliates**, the clip will be added to the multiclip in the Viewer *and* to any multiclips you've edited down to the Timeline.

● EXTRA CREDIT

To shuffle the order of images in the Viewer, press the **Command** key and drag them into a new position.

To remove an angle from a multiclip, press the **Command** key and drag it out of the Viewer window.

Match Frames and Multiclips
Match frames for multiclips are just like match frames for clips—sort of.

In the same way we can find match frames for individual clips and subclips, we can do the same for multiclips—we just have more choices.

To match a Browser source clip to a multiclip angle in the Timeline:

- Put your playhead in the angle you want to find and press **F** (**View > Match Frame > Master Clip**). The source clip appears in the Viewer, matching the position of the playhead.

To find the location of the Browser source clip:

- Put your playhead in the angle you want to find and select **View > Match Frame > Multi-clip Angle**.

To match an active multiclip angle in the Viewer to a multiclip in the Timeline:

1. Double-click the source clip in the Browser to load it into the Viewer (this replaces any multiclips that may be there).
2. Select **View > Match Frame > Multiclip Angle**. The Timeline playhead jumps to the matching frame that's displayed in the Viewer.

Multiclip Mishaps
Not all multiclips are created equal...

Having problems with getting a multiclip to work properly?

Keep in mind that all source clips for a multiclip need to be the same video format, the same frame size, and the same frame rate. In other words, they need to be technically identical.

● **EXTRA CREDIT**

To rebuild a collapsed multiclip for editing, select the multi-clip and choose **Modify > Uncollapse Multiclip**.

● **NOTE**

Remember to select **Modify > Collapse Multiclip** to collapse your multiclip when you are done editing it to minimize wear and tear on your hard drives. This tells Final Cut to play only the data it needs, not all the linked clips of a multiclip.

Getting Multiclips to Play Properly
Multiclips require a really fast hard drive—and a special RT setting.

If you plan to do a lot of multiclip work, getting a fast hard drive—or, far better, a RAID—should be part of your plan. While you can easily handle four to five DV streams for a multiclip, many HD formats require far faster data streams.

There's also an RT menu setting that can make a difference in whether your multiclips play smoothly.

Before starting your multiclip, open the RT menu in the top-left corner of the Timeline and set the following:

- Unlimited RT
- Dynamic image quality
- Dynamic frame rate

This allows Final Cut Pro to modify both the frame rate and image quality *during editing* and so minimizes the load on your CPU. This setting doesn't affect output, only editing, so you can change it as often as you wish.

> ● **NOTE**
>
> Changing the RT menu does not affect the data rate you need from your hard disk; it only affects how the processor handles the data. So if you are getting dropped frame errors during playback, the most likely solution will be a faster hard disk, not changing this menu.

CHAPTER 6

Audio

Picture is important, but good audio is essential.

People will happily watch low-quality images as long as the audio is good. YouTube is the classic proof of that.

Yet, far too often, audio is given short shrift during production. "Oh, we'll fix that in post" is a statement heard all too often on the set. Taking a couple of extra minutes to get a good clean recording on set can save hours of expensive repair work later—and often yields far better results.

But since this book is written for editors, you already know that. So now the question becomes, "How do I get my audio to sound good in Final Cut Pro?"

That's what this chapter is all about.

Two Types of Audio Files
You can capture audio into Final Cut Pro in one of two ways.

There are two ways you can capture, or ingest, audio into Final Cut Pro:

- **Dual-channel mono** (tracks 1 and 2 in the screen shot) means there is no audio level link between the two tracks. Both tracks are panned center and the audio levels between the two clips are independent. Both tracks are, however, locked together for sync.

- **Stereo** (tracks 3 and 4) means there is a link between the two tracks. The top track is panned left, the bottom track is panned right, and the audio levels of the two tracks are linked so that as you raise or lower one, the other moves by the same amount.

You can easily change the mode by clicking the little "cassette" icon, to the left of the tracks, to toggle from one mode to the other.

You should use dual-channel mono audio for interviews; this puts one person speaking on one channel, with the interviewer on the other channel. For most interviews, narration, and other one-person audio, there is no need for stereo.

You should use stereo settings for music, or sound effects, or in those situations where you care about the placement of sound in space.

Monitoring Audio and Video in Sync
Before you start blaming Final Cut Pro, read this first.

Although there are a few reasons why your audio and video may be playing out of sync, the most common reason is operator error. The golden rule of monitoring is: be sure you are listening to your audio and video from the same point.

If you send video out Final Cut via FireWire to an external deck or camera, you must monitor audio from the same deck or camera. This is because FireWire—and interconnection cards

from companies like AJA, Blackmagic Design, Matrox, and Aurora—creates a signal-processing delay going through your gear that can range from three to nine frames.

If you plug your speakers into your computer and watch your video on a monitor attached to your deck, the sound will be out of sync. The way to fix this is to be sure audio and video monitors are both connected to the same source.

Understanding Sample Rates
Sample rates determine the frequency response of your audio.

Frequency response is the ability of your audio recordings to accurately capture all the different sounds in your recording. Normal human hearing is described as ranging from 20 cycles per second (extremely deep bass) to 20,000 cycles (extremely high pitch). Twenty cycles is so deep it sounds more like a vibration than a tone; 20,000 cycles is so high it sounds more like wind in the trees than a pitch.

Audio is analog, and in almost all cases it is created from something vibrating, setting up pressure waves that float through the air until heard by your ear. However, computers are digital and dislike all things analog.

We use sampling, which means capturing and measuring very small time slices of sound, to convert an analog signal into a digital format. According to the Nyquist Theorem (which I know you remember from high school physics), if you divide the sample rate by 2, you get the maximum frequency response supported by a particular sample rate.

All sample rates adequately capture low-frequency sounds—provided they can be picked up by your microphone. The following table illustrates frequency ranges of popular sample rates.

NOTE
Your ear will not hear frequencies greater than 20,000 Hz.

FREQUENCY RANGES FOR POPULAR SAMPLE RATES

Description	Sample Rate	Frequency Response
Normal human hearing	N/A	20–20,000 Hz
Human speech	N/A	300–7,500 Hz (Guys slightly lower, girls slightly higher)
Poor AM radio	11.025 kHz	20–5,512 Hz
Near FM radio	22.050 kHz	20–11,025 Hz
Better than FM radio	32 kHz	20–16,000 Hz
CD audio	44.1 kHz	20–22,050 Hz
Standard DVD and video recording	48 kHz	20–24,000 Hz
High-end audio processing	96 kHz	20–48,000 Hz

Understanding Bit Depth
Bit depth determines dynamic range.

Dynamic range is the difference between the loudest and softest portions of your audio. When dynamic range is great, there is a large difference between volume levels.

Bit depth determines how much volume information the computer can record. All bit depths set the maximum level at the same point. Varying the bit depth determines how soft the quietest portions can be.

Final Cut Pro supports four principal bit depth settings:

- **8-bit depth** allows a dynamic range from 0 dB (as loud as your audio can be) to –96 dB. This range creates smaller file sizes and is a common format for the Web.

- **16-bit depth** allows a dynamic range from 0 dB (which is the same level as 8-bit) to –124 dB. This is the standard for almost all video-recording gear.

- **24-bit depth** allows a dynamic range from 0 dB to –143 dB. This is currently common in professional audio gear and high-end mixing.

- **32-bit depth** is the internal resolution of the Final Cut Pro mixer.

In all cases, increased bit depth does not change how loud your audio can be. Instead, it allows softer and softer sounds to be recorded.

NOTE
The larger the bit depth, the larger the file size.

NOTE
Final Cut Pro displays audio using dBFS, where 0 is as loud as your audio can go. All audio levels below that are represented as negative numbers.

Is Your Audio Slowly Drifting Out of Sync?

The problem is not in your set—it's in your capture.

If your audio starts in sync with your video and then slowly drifts more and more out of sync, the problem isn't your ears. It's how you shot and captured the clip.

By default, Final Cut Pro expects all audio to be recorded by a camera with a 48 kHz sample rate (48,000 cycles per second). The problem is that many of the less expensive consumer cameras record audio at 32 kHz. When Final Cut Pro captures the clip, it flags the audio at the wrong sample rate, which causes the drift.

You need to do two things:

- Change your audio capture settings and recapture the clip.

- Change your camera settings so that all future recordings are done at the proper 48 kHz sample rate.

To change your capture settings, make sure your camera or deck is connected and turned on; then follow these steps:

1. Choose **Final Cut Pro > Audio/Video Settings** and click the **Capture Preset** tab.

2. Select the preset that has a check mark (meaning it is your currently active setting) and duplicate it.

3. If the Settings dialog box does not open, click the **Edit** button.

4. At the top, give this setting a name you'll remember, like "Capture 32 kHz audio." At the bottom, under QuickTime Audio Settings, change Format to 32.000 kHz.

5. Click **OK**.

6. In the Capture Presets tab, select your newly created setting and click **OK**.

Remember to use Easy Setup to change back to your normal capture setting when you are done capturing this footage.

To change your camera record settings, select the Camera menu and change it to record audio at either 48 kHz or, for some cameras, 16-bit.

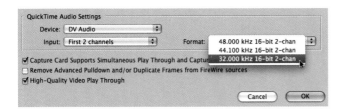

Adjusting for Playback Latency

Here's the fix when your external monitor is out of sync with your computer.

The Power Skill on page 154 mentioned that you need to connect your audio and video to the same monitoring point. However, it's still possible for your computer and external monitor to be out of sync.

That's because there's an inherent delay, called *latency*, present in any digital signal path. Final Cut Pro compensates for this inside the computer. But you may need to adjust this for monitoring outside the computer.

For example, if your video monitor shows your program six frames later than your computer display, a Frame Offset value of 6 will synchronize the computer screen with your external video monitor.

Adjust for the delay between your computer and an external device by choosing **Final Cut Pro > System Settings** and selecting the **Playback Control** tab. On this tab, you'll see the **Frame Offset** setting. (Frame Offset is only active when Final Cut Pro is handling real-time effects.)

The default value is 4, but Frame Offset can be any whole number between 0 and 30. Set a value that compensates for any delay in your setup. For example, if your video monitor shows your program six frames later than your computer display, a Frame Offset value of **6** will synchronize the two.

NOTE

Frame Offset adjusts audio and video equally. If your audio is out of sync, changing the frame offset will not bring it back into sync.

EXTRA CREDIT

A quick way to test for sync is to put a short, one-frame pop of bars and tone every few seconds in the Timeline. Play this test sequence back and adjust the Frame Offset setting until the bars and tone sound in sync between the computer and external monitors.

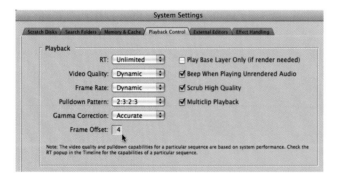

Toggling Audio Waveforms
Waveforms display visually the volume of your audio. Here's how to turn them on or off.

The keyboard shortcut to show, or hide, audio waveforms in the Timeline is **Option+Command+W**. This toggles waveform display on or off.

Displaying audio waveforms in your Timeline takes time because Final Cut Pro must redraw them on your screen. This means that when you are working with longer and longer sequences, every time you zoom the Timeline, or scroll it to a different position, audio waveforms will need time to redraw.

So when you're not editing audio, or if you're displaying a very large sequence, screen redraws will take place faster with waveforms turned off.

● **EXTRA CREDIT**

You can also toggle audio waveforms on or off with the mouse by clicking the small, right-pointing arrow next to the bar chart at the bottom left of the Timeline and selecting the option from the pop-up menu.

● **NOTE**

Toggling waveforms on or off has no effect on audio quality.

Sync Audio to Video in Real Time
Here's a fast way to sync sound to picture.

They shot double system—your audio is in one file and the video is in another. They didn't use clapper slates, so you can't line up the clapper slate video with the sound of the clapper in the audio. "You can fix it in post," they said.

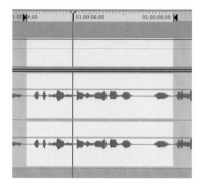

Here's how to marry up the audio between the two files—in real time:

1. Select the clip, audio or video, that you want to move; generally, we slip the audio clip. (Press the **Option** key to select just the audio clip.)

2. Select the Slip tool by pressing **S**.

3. Mark In and Out points in the Timeline that includes a good sync point, like a hand clap or something dropping—in other words, something that generates a sharp sound.

4. Select **View > Loop Playback** (or press **Control+L**).

5. Press **Shift+** to play from the In to the Out point. The selected range loops playback while you adjust the position of the audio.

6. Press **[** and **]** to slip the selected clip one frame at a time until the audio and video are in sync. Press **Shift+[** or **Shift+]** to slip five frames at a time.

● **EXTRA CREDIT**

You can also use the **period** and **comma** keys, or **Shift-period** and **Shift-comma** to move the clip.

● **NOTE**

It's a good idea to use Clip markers to keep track of where you started.

It's Becoming Visible

What's the difference between the green visibility light and the Mute/Solo buttons?

Ever wonder why both these sets of buttons exist on the left of the Timeline? Well, it's because they do different things. The green visibility lights permanently affect output. If the light is on (green), the track will play back and output normally. If the light is dark, the track acts as though it's invisible. Clips on invisible tracks don't output to tape, export, render, or play back during editing.

Changing the status of one of these lights permanently deletes all render files associated with that track. (Yes, you can get them back with an Undo—and there is a warning message—but aside from that, the deletion is permanent.)

The Mute and Solo buttons are only temporary for editing playback purposes. They don't affect output or export or render files. Click the **Mute** button (the speaker icon) to make an audio track inaudible. Click the **Solo** button (the headset icon) to make every track *except* the track(s) soloed inaudible.

You can mute or solo as many different tracks as you need. If you forget to turn one of these buttons off, that track will still export with your project.

● **NOTE**

Can't see the Mute or Solo buttons? Click the tiny, little speaker icon in the extreme lower-left corner of the Timeline.

● **EXTRA CREDIT**

Try Option-clicking one of the green visibility lights. This is a very fast way to turn all other tracks off, or turn them all on again.

More on Mute and Solo Audio Buttons
The Mute and Solo buttons make tracks audible or inaudible.

Yes, you can turn off, or on, the green visibility lights to the left of the Timeline to make an audio track inaudible. You can also choose **Modify > Clip Enable**. But whenever you change these green lights, they delete all render files associated with the clips on that track.

That's because you're making a permanent change to the output settings for that sequence. Render files are associated with the sequence, not the clips *in* the sequence.

However, the Mute and Solo buttons only affect playback settings during editing. Since they don't permanently change output settings, no render files are lost.

To mute all the clips on a track, click the small speaker button.

To solo all clips on a track, click the small headset button.

● **EXTRA CREDIT**

Pressing Option while clicking the Mute (or Solo) button quickly turns all Mute (or Solo) buttons on or off. This is a fast way to reset these settings.

Counting Words to Estimate Voice-Over Timing
This chart helps you figure out how long a script will take to read.

Gregory Ikens sent me this tip. The following word count timings can assist you in determining how many words will comfortably fit within a specified amount of time in a spot. This guide assumes a "normal" rate of speech (neither fast nor slow) and a basic "announcer" read.

Note that for phone numbers, each spoken number equals one word (i.e., 1-877-000-0000 = 11 words).

WORD COUNT TIMINGS

Words	Seconds
7 words	3 seconds
12 words	5 seconds
17 words	7 seconds
23 words	10 seconds
35 words	15 seconds
70 words	30 seconds
140 words	60 seconds

Shortcut to Solo a Track

Here's a fast way to solo an entire audio track with one keyboard shortcut.

Soloing is the process of making all audio tracks inaudible except the one you solo. You can do this with the Mute and Solo buttons, as already discussed, but here's a fast way to do it with a keyboard shortcut.

Select a clip in the track you want to solo (that is, the tracks you want to hear) and press **Control+S**. This is similar to turning off clip visibility for a video clip (**Control+B**).

To toggle everything back to normal, select something in the same track and press **Control+S** again.

> **NOTE**
> Using this keyboard shortcut does not change the Mute and Solo indicators on the left side of the Timeline.

> **NOTE**
> This also makes any linked video clips invisible.

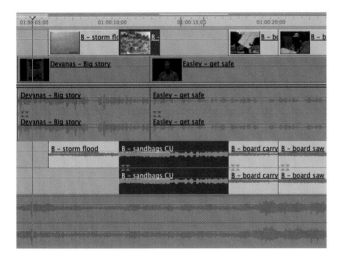

Picking the Best Audio Transition
0 dB or +3 dB Cross-Fade—which is better?

Final Cut Pro has a vast plethora of visual transitions… and exactly two transitions for audio. Both of these audio transitions have names. The 0 dB transition is called Equal Power, while the +3 dB transition is called Equal Gain. Here's how to pick.

Audio gain, also called audio level, is logarithmic—as volume increases it has the shape of a hockey stick, not a straight line. When you cross-fade between two clips, if you don't compensate for this, there will be a slight decrease in audio gain in the middle of the cross-fade. Specifically, the audio level drops 3 dB.

So, if you're dissolving from one audio clip to the next, and both have fairly constant levels of sound (such as machine noise or enthusiastic crickets), use the +3 dB cross-fade to smooth out the levels and make the transition seamless.

If you're fading to or from black, you will probably find that the 0 dB cross-fade sounds the smoothest.

EXTRA CREDIT

Final Cut Pro has two audio transitions, but Soundtrack Pro has four. Even better, you can change the transition shape at each end of the clip. For most purposes, these two in Final Cut Pro will be fine. But for greater control, Soundtrack Pro is the better choice.

NOTE

It's because of the logarithmic nature of audio gain that when we use keyframes to set clip audio levels using the red bands in the Timeline, the lines between audio keyframes are curved. This is also the reason we can't add Beziér curves to audio keyframes.

That Hidden Voice Over Tool

The Voice Over tool in Final Cut Pro helps you make quick recordings.

Built into Final Cut Pro is a voice-over recorder. This is a great tool for recording narration scratch tracks or quick reports in the field. To use it:

1. Set In and Out points in your Timeline where you want the new recording to go.

2. Select **Tools > Voice Over** (press **Option+0**).

3. Set your audio source using the Source and Input pop-ups.

4. If you are using headsets, check **Sound Cues**; otherwise deselect this option to keep your audio clean. (Sound cues are audible beeps that help you time your reading.)

5. Click the red Record button to start recording. The tool counts you down to the In point and then again to the Out. During recording it plays your sequence so you can watch what you are talking about.

Final Cut puts the audio file between the In and Out points on the first open audio track in your project.

● **NOTE**

The Voice Over tool records several seconds before and one second after the In and Out points. That way, in case you blew the cue your complete audio is still recorded.

● **EXTRA CREDIT**

Ever wonder where those voice-over recordings are stored? Well, you can find them in your scratch disk—specifically, in your Capture Scratch folder in the folder named after your project. The path is...Final Cut Pro Documents > Capture Scratch > Project folder > [Voice-Over Recording File].

Checkerboard Your Audio Clips

You have to edit your clips into the Timeline someplace—why not edit them in an organized fashion?

Audio checkerboarding is the process of putting similar clips on the same track. The benefit to checkerboarding is that, while Final Cut Pro doesn't particularly care which tracks your clips are on, ProTools and Soundtrack Pro care a lot. For this reason, get into the habit of following the same organizational structure for your audio clips.

● **EXTRA CREDIT**

If you don't have a particular audio source, such as sound effects, simply move the lower tracks higher. But keep this stacking order intact.

There are three benefits to this:

1. You'll never need to invent a new system. You'll know exactly how you structured your audio even on projects that are several years old.

2. Your audio will be laid out properly for transfer to ProTools or Soundtrack Pro, if you need a professional mix.

3. This system fits well with the way Final Cut Pro works.

Here's the layout:

- **A1 & A2:** Sync sound linked to the video clips on V1. This is the audio from your main speaker, the main talking head.

- **A3 & A4**: Sync sound linked to the B-roll on V2; natural sound.

- **A5**: Narrator. The narrator only needs one track because they have only one voice.

- **A6–A8**: Sound effects. These are wild sounds, not linked to any track. (Wild means not synced to video. That doesn't mean they are placed haphazardly.)

- **A9 & A10**: Music cue #1.

- **A11 & A12**: Music cue #2. Alternating music cues between tracks allows you to easily control the speed of fade-ins and fade-outs independently.

Setting Audio Levels
There's no one perfect set of levels, but these are a good place to start.

Camera people like arguing about cameras. Lighting people like arguing about lights. And audio people really like, ah, "discussing" audio levels. Different programs are mixed to different levels, and there's plenty of room for disagreement.

Mixing to the right audio levels is critical to the sound of your project. Over the years, I've taught this system and it works. If you're given specific written instructions on how to mix your project, please follow them. If not, use these:

- **Rule 1:** Audio levels must not, ever, for any reason, exceed 0 dB.

- **Rule 2:** Reread Rule #1.

- **Rule 3:** Audio levels should be as loud as possible, without violating Rule #1.

Audio levels are additive. The more audio clips that are playing at the same time, the louder your total audio will be. Given that fact, here are the levels I mix to.

● **NOTE**
How quiet your audio goes is an aesthetic decision you get to make. Just remember that at no time can your audio levels exceed 0 dB.

● **NOTE**
Exceeding 0 dB is indicated on your VU meters by red clip lights at the top of the meter. Clipping creates distortion, which makes your audio sound awful. Always avoid distortion and keep your levels below 0 dB.

GUIDELINE FOR AUDIO MIXING

Content	Level on Audio Meters
Total mix	−3 to −6 dB
Main audio source (e.g., interview)	−6 to −12 dB
Natural sound and sound effects	−12 to −18 dB
Underscored music	−18 dB

The only level that's critical is the Total Mix. I use these other levels to roughly adjust my audio during editing. Then, I use my good speakers, my good ears, and my good common sense to tweak all these settings to make it all sound right, within the range of the Total Mix.

No Red Lights

Final Cut Pro has three technical settings that you must get right. Audio levels are one of them...

... and the other two are white levels and chroma levels. You'll learn about those in the next chapter.

In this chapter, though, we are talking about audio.

In Final Cut, all audio levels are clip-based. That is, you set levels individually for each clip. By contrast, professional audio mixing software, such as Soundtrack Pro or ProTools, sets audio levels by track, not clip.

In the last Power Skill you learned that the number one rule for audio is that levels must not exceed 0 dB. We have many ways of measuring audio. Final Cut's audio meters use the dBFS (Decibel Full Scale) method, which is typically used in digital audio. The good thing about this scale is that it consistently, and reliably, measures audio levels. The bad thing is that any audio that exceeds 0 dB is thrown away. Lost. Destroyed.

The result of losing this audio is distortion. In an analog system, distortion has a nice buzz that sounds good on guitars. In a digital environment, distortion pops, clicks, crackles, and gives the same feeling as fingernails scraping across a blackboard.

Worse, if you output or export distorted audio there is not a technology on the planet that can fix it. The data is lost; your audio has been permanently destroyed.

To prevent this problem, pay attention to your levels and always keep them below 0 dB.

● **NOTE**

Audio levels are measured by the audio meter. If the red clip indicators at the top of the meter light, as shown here, your audio is too loud (this is also known as audio that is too "hot"). Adjust the audio levels of your clips to make sure the red indicators never light.

Boosting Low Audio: Method 1
Here's a quick tip to boost soft audio.

This trick has been around for a long time because it works (though, as you'll see next, more recent versions of Final Cut offer an easier way).

If you have an audio clip that was recorded at too low a level, simply cranking up the volume won't give you the loudness you're looking for. Instead, try "stacking" the audio clip(s) to bring up the overall volume level. The easiest way to do this is to **Shift+Option-drag** the audio clip you want to improve.

In the screen shot, notice how the upper clip is underlined, meaning it's linked to the video clip. The other two copies are not, meaning they are copies of the linked clip. Holding the Shift key constrains movement so the clip doesn't shift from side to side, creating an echo effect.

● **NOTE**

Recently, Apple added a Normalize command that does a better job. The next Power Skill talks about that.

Boosting Low Audio: Method 2
Normalizing audio is faster than duplicating clips and does a safer job.

Remember Rule #1—that audio levels must never exceed 0 dB?

Well, if you're raising or lowering volume levels, or duplicating clips to make audio levels louder, there's nothing to prevent you from pushing the gain so hard (translation: "raising the audio level to such an amount") that your audio distorts.

This would be bad.

Recent versions of Final Cut Pro added a new feature: normalization. Normalization is defined as raising the level of the entire audio clip by the same amount so that the loudest portion of the clip does not exceed the level that you specify.

Normalization is designed so that it's impossible for your clip to distort. This means you can quickly raise the level of an entire range of clips so they all have the same level without worry. Here's how:

1. Select all the audio clips you want to normalize. Generally, you only normalize talking head audio. I recommend against normalizing sound effects or music.
2. Select **Modify > Audio > Apply Normalization Gain**.
3. Here's the tricky part:
   - If the clips you are normalizing are the only clips playing at that moment in your sequence, for example, and there are no sound effects or music playing at the same time, normalize to **–3 dBFS**.
   - If the clips you are normalizing are part of a mix, with many clips playing at once, then normalize to **– 4.5 dBFS**. This lower level allows room in the mix for other audio to be heard.
4. Click **OK**, and almost instantly the levels of all your selected clips are normalized to the same level.

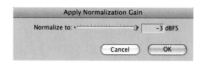

NOTE

Final Cut Pro applies a Gain filter to each clip, which is why you don't see the waveforms change, as you'd expect.

Changing Audio Levels Fast!

This keyboard shortcut lets you change audio levels in the Timeline.

Here's a quick way to adjust audio levels using only the keyboard:

1. Select the clip, or clips, you want to adjust. (You can even do this for clips on multiple tracks.)

2. Press one of the following four keyboard shortcuts:

Raise audio levels +3 dB	**Control+]**
Raise audio levels +1 dB	**Control+=**
Lower audio levels –1 dB	**Control+-**
Lower audio levels –3 dB	**Control+[**

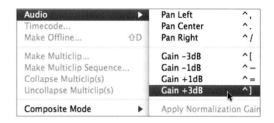

● **NOTE**
Remember, after adjusting levels listen to your clips and watch the audio meters to be *sure* your levels aren't too loud.

Changing Audio Levels Faster!

Here's another quick way to adjust the audio levels of multiple clips.

The last Power Skill used keyboard shortcuts; this one uses a menu:

1. Select the audio clips whose level you want to adjust.

2. Choose **Modify > Level** (or press **Option+Command+L**).

3. Select **Relative** if you want to adjust the levels of each clip based on the current settings of the clip. Select **Absolute** if you want to set the level of all clips to the same setting, regardless of where the audio is set now.

4. Enter the amount you want to change the audio (negative numbers make sounds quieter; positive numbers make it louder).

5. Click **OK**.

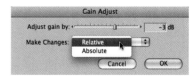

● **NOTE**
This is a good way to drop the level of all the selected clips, such as sound effects, in a sequence by the same amount.

In general, the Relative setting should be tried first.

One More Way to Adjust Levels
Just in case you were wondering...

You can also adjust audio levels directly in the Timeline. To turn on Timeline audio levels, click the small black mountain range in the lower-left corner (Apple calls this the **Clip Overlay** button).

This displays red rubber bands over all your audio clips. Drag the rubber bands up or down to set levels for each clip.

This is the audio level setting technique that I use the most.

> **NOTE**
> You can use the Pen tool (press **P**) to set keyframes for these audio levels.

● **EXTRA CREDIT**
You can also adjust audio levels for a clip in the Viewer by double-clicking a timeline clip to load it into the Viewer, then dragging the red rubber band; adjusting the Level slider; or entering a value in the Level data entry box.

Locate Audio Levels That Are Too Loud
Here's how to spot problems.

Remember Rule #1: Audio levels in Final Cut should never go above 0 dB. The red clip lights in the audio meters must not glow. But how can you be sure without listening to your sequence over and over?

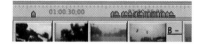

Here's a quick way to check your sequence.

1. Either select the Timeline containing your sequence or drag the sequence from the Browser into the Viewer.
2. Choose **Mark > Audio Peaks > Mark**.
3. Final Cut quickly scans your sequence and puts either an orange (Final Cut Pro 7) or a green marker (Final Cut Pro 6) wherever it finds audio levels that are too loud.
4. These markers are stored in the sequence. If it isn't already in the Timeline, open the sequence in the Timeline.

> **NOTE**
> The cool thing about this technique is that you see your audio problems instantly, and the audio markers are easily cleared from the Timeline without disturbing your other markers.

5. Press **Shift+M** or **Option+M** to jump from marker to marker and adjust the audio levels accordingly.
6. To delete all these audio markers in the Timeline, choose **Mark > Audio Peaks > Clear**.

What Do Pan Numbers Mean?

Panning adjusts the amount of audio that comes out of the left or right speaker.

Panning determines the balance between sounds coming out the left speaker and the right speaker. As you know, there are two types of audio clips inside Final Cut Pro: stereo and mono.

A *stereo* clip consists of two linked clips stored on two separate tracks. (Final Cut always places multitrack audio on separate tracks.) The top clip, the left channel, plays exclusively from the left speaker. The bottom clip, the right channel, plays exclusively from the right speaker. The audio levels between the two clips are linked, meaning that if you adjust one clip, the other side adjusts by the same amount. A stereo clip is indicated by the two small green "bowties" pointing between the two tracks.

A *mono* clip consists of at least one track of audio. By default, a mono track plays equally from both the left and right speaker (we call this "panned center").

For a stereo clip:

- A Pan setting of **–1** means the left channel comes out the left speaker and the right chan-nel comes out the right speaker—the channels are normal.
- A Pan setting of **0** means both channels ema-nate equally from both speakers—thus giving the illusion of all audio placed in the center.
- A Pan setting of **+1** means the left channel comes out the right speaker and the right channel comes out the left speaker—the chan-nels cross.

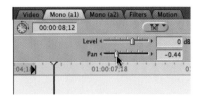

● **NOTE**
Both stereo and mono audio tracks can be synced to a video clip. The audio setting has no effect on sync.

For a mono clip:

- A Pan setting of **–1** means the track comes exclusively out the left speaker.
- A Pan setting of **0** means the track comes equally out both left and right speakers.
- A Pan setting of **+1** means the track comes exclusively out the right speaker.

Sliding the Pan setting between these extremes moves your sound around the sonic field between the two speakers.

The Quickest Way to Pan Audio for Multiple Clips
Blindingly fast, super easy.

In Final Cut Pro, you can only incrementally adjust Pan settings clip by clip.

However, here's a neat trick to shift the pan absolutely to the full left, right, or center for a single clip or group of clips.

Open your sequence in the Timeline and select all the clips you want to pan to one side. Then choose **Modify > Audio** and then select:

- **Pan Left** (or press **Control+,**) to pan all select clips fully to the left.

- **Pan Center** (or press **Control+.**) to pan all select clips fully to the center.

- **Pan Right** (or press **Control+/**) to pan all select clips fully to the right.

> ● **NOTE**
> If you looked at your keyboard and discovered that the comma key is on the left, the period key is in the middle, and the slash key is on the right, give yourself a gold star.

Mixed Panning on Multiple Clips
Here's a fast way to adjust Pan or Gain across a selection of clips.

All audio settings in Final Cut Pro are clip based. This is both a great strength, because working with individual clips is easy, and a serious weakness, because working with lots of individual clips is time-consuming.

Unless you know this trick…

Once you have the audio mix set for one clip that you want to apply equally to other clips, select the clip with the correct settings and then choose **Edit > Copy** (or press **Command+C**) to copy the attributes of the clip.

Next, select the clips you want to apply these audio settings to and choose **Edit > Paste Attributes** (or press **Option+V**), select the **Pan** check box under Audio Attributes, and then click **OK**.

● **EXTRA CREDIT**

You can use the same technique of pasting attributes to set matching audio levels across multiple clips. Just remember to select the Levels check box in Paste Attributes.

Discover the Final Cut Pro Audio Mixer
Did you know there's an audio mixer buried in Final Cut Pro?

Final Cut has an audio mixer complete with audio meters, level sliders, and pan controls hidden in it that can greatly simplify mixing your projects. The only problem is that it's hidden.

To access the mixer you can select **Tools > Audio Mixer**, which places the mixer on top of the Viewer. But a much better way is to choose **Window > Arrange > Audio Mixing** because this rearranges all your windows to make room for the mixer.

The benefit to using the mixer is that you can adjust levels in real time, which you can't do when adjusting the red rubber bands. With the mixer, you can mix sound on the fly like you would with a mixing board!

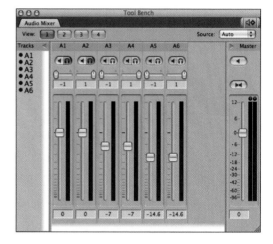

● NOTE

The Mute and Solo buttons are duplicated from the side of the Timeline into the top of the Mixer. They work exactly the same way.

Automatically Record Audio-Level Keyframes
Tired of creating audio keyframes by hand? You don't have to!

The greatest strength in using the audio mixer is almost impossible to find. It has the ability to automatically record audio-level keyframes in real time during playback!

1. Choose **Window > Arrange > Audio Mixing**.

2. In the top-right corner of the audio mixer is a gray button with a speaker and a diamond keyframe icon. When you click it (so it turns green), auto-keyframing is turned on.

3. Play your sequence and move the audio sliders in the mixer as you listen to your project. Final Cut automatically records keyframes based on how you move the sliders.

4. To turn off auto-keyframing, click the button again so it goes gray.

Being able to hear your mix while mixing it is a great time-saver!

● **EXTRA CREDIT**

You can adjust, move, and delete any keyframes recorded this way the same as always—by grabbing them in the Timeline with your mouse and moving them, or by using the Pen tool.

● **NOTE**

Final Cut Pro also supports using external control surfaces for mixing. Similar to a traditional mixer, but connected to the computer, you can move faders and dials on the control surface to mix your audio in Final Cut. The Mackie Control Universal Pro (www.mackie.com) is probably the best known of these control surfaces.

The Hidden Value of Mixdown

When nesting sequences, this is an essential audio step.

Final Cut Pro allows up to eight levels of nesting, or putting sequences inside other sequences. However, when you nest your audio Final Cut sometimes gets confused, resulting in missing audio or bad audio levels.

Whenever you start creating nests composed of both audio and video, make a point to select **Sequence > Render Only > Mixdown** (or press **Option+Command+R**).

What this does is mix all the audio in all sequences into a single stereo pair. This reduces the load on the processor and results in cleaner audio playback.

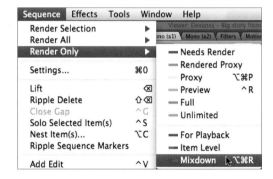

● **EXTRA CREDIT**

Feel free to use Mixdown whenever you have lots of audio tracks in a project, even if you don't nest. Mixdown will always result in smoother playback.

● **NOTE**

Mixdowns are temporary. If you change any audio clips or settings, all existing mixdown files are automatically deleted. There's nothing you need to manage—Final Cut Pro does it for you.

Adjusting Audio Filters in Real Time
Setting audio filter parameters during playback is easy.

Is there an audio filter you want to try, but you're not sure of the best setting to use?

Well, this is a great way to experiment—in real time:

1. For better audio "visibility," press **Option+Command+W** to see the waveforms for your audio clip.

2. Select the clip and choose **Effects > Audio Filters > Final Cut Pro > Reverberation** (or whatever effect you want to apply to the clip).

3. Set In and Out points to represent the duration you want to review.

4. Double-click the clip to load it into the Viewer and click the **Filters** tab.

5. Choose **View > Loop Playback** and make sure Loop Playback has a check mark beside it.

6. Press **Shift+** to start your sequence. Adjust the effect parameters of your choice in the Viewer, in real time, while listening to your clip.

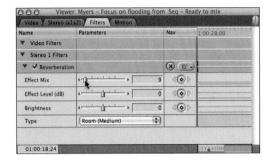

● **NOTE**

Given a choice, I prefer the quality of audio filters from the Final Cut Pro group rather than those from Apple. However, if I have the time, I will always do significant audio processing in Soundtrack Pro, which has far superior audio filters and controls compared to Final Cut Pro.

Creating Multiple Track Audio Output
Final Cut Pro supports up to 24 audio tracks for output.

By default, Final Cut creates a single stereo pair for audio output of our finished projects. However, Final Cut allows us to create up to 24 discrete tracks for audio output using **Sequence > Settings > Audio Outputs**. In this example, I've switched from the default setting of stereo (2 tracks) to 8 tracks for output.

Final Cut always creates audio output tracks in pairs. Once you've set the number of tracks in this dialog box, you also need to set whether each track is a stereo pair or a dual-channel mono.

When you click **OK**, a dialog box pops up asking if you want to downmix. This means that you will output multiple tracks, but monitor them during editing as a single stereo pair. If you don't have multichannel hardware to hear all these tracks, downmixing is a good idea.

Once you've created the number of output tracks you need, you still must assign each Final Cut Pro audio track to an output—which you'll learn in the next Power Skill.

● **NOTE**

A good example of when to use multichannel output is when you need to output a finished mix as *stems*, where the dialogue is on one stereo pair, effects on a second stereo pair, and music on a third stereo pair.

● **NOTE**

Notice how the level setting changes in this dialog box depending on whether you are outputting stereo or dual-channel mono. This 3 dB setting change is correct and compensates for the differences in the combined signal strength of a stereo pair versus individual tracks. My suggestion is to leave these settings alone.

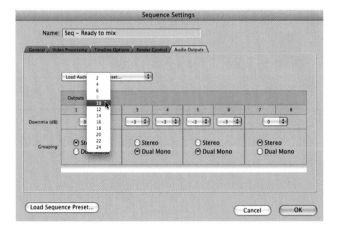

Assigning Tracks to Audio Channels
For multichannel output, you need to assign each track to an output channel.

Once we set up multiple track output, we now need to assign each audio track in the Timeline to a specific output channel. Finding this setting, however, is completely unintuitive.

Control-click in the gray area *between* the audio patch and the track lock for each track. There's no yellow tool tip to warn you; you just do this on faith.

From the pop-up menu, select **Audio Output**, then select the output channel(s) you want to assign that track to. This pop-up menu changes depending on how you configure the Audio Output settings we showed you in the last Power Skill.

Can't Hear Audio on Even-Numbered Tracks?
It's simply a setting in the wrong place.

Peter Koeleman sent me this tip. He was having a problem with hearing the audio on even tracks (2, 4, 6,…), no matter which camera he used.

Peter determined that it was simply a sequence setting that was incorrectly set to Mono. To fix this, he says, simply choose **Sequence > Settings > Audio Output > Stereo**. To get the output you expect, be sure Outputs is set to **2** tracks and Grouping is set to **Stereo**.

It's great to hear what you were missing.

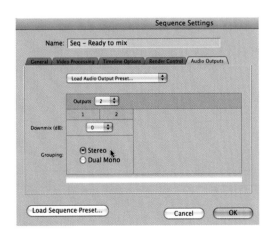

Creating Split Track Audio

Here's how to create a split-track audio output from Final Cut Pro.

If you need to create split track audio where, say, dialogue is on the odd track with music and effects on the even track (which simplifies dialogue editing, or for news archiving), Final Cut makes it easy:

1. Open the sequence you want to change.

2. Choose **Sequence > Settings > Audio Output**.

3. From the pop-up menu, select the number of tracks you need to output.

4. Set each track to **Dual Mono**, which pans both tracks center, as opposed to the default setting of Stereo. (By the way, the gain reduction on each track of –3 dB is appropriate and should be left alone.)

5. Output your sequence.

● **EXTRA CREDIT**

If you plan to do this on a regular basis, you can make this a preference setting so that every new sequence is configured this way. The Power Skill on the next page shows you how.

Resetting Multiple Audio Outputs

Resetting audio output tracks is time-consuming, unless…

Shane Ross sent me this tip. Let's say you have a source file with eight tracks of audio, and you mapped a1 and a2 to A7 and A8 on the Timeline, and a5 is pointing to A6… In other words, the track assignments are *all* over the place.

To get your tracks back to the proper order could take dozens of clicks; which is very time consuming! But you can just Control-click in the gray area anywhere in the left side of the Timeline and select the **Reset Panel** option.

All audio outputs pop back into order, and everything is properly connected.

● **NOTE**

This same pop-up menu allows you add and delete tracks as well. There is all kinds of hidden stuff in this application.

Changing Preferences for Split Track Audio
You can modify preferences to create multichannel audio.

So far, all our audio output changes are for individual sequences. But, if you need all your sequences to have the same value, it makes more sense to change this in preferences.

For example, to create split track audio where, say, dialogue is on the odd track with music and effects on the even track (or any other non-stereo track output), Final Cut's Preferences make it possible. Here's how:

1. Select **Final Cut Pro > User Preferences > Audio Output**.

2. Click the **Duplicate** button to make a copy of whatever sequence is highlighted. (Apple does not allow us to change their default Stereo Monitoring setting.)

3. Give the new setting a name and a description so you can remember what you did later.

4. Make the audio output changes you need.

5. When done, click **OK**, which saves the settings.

6. In the main preferences window, select the audio output setting you want to use for all new projects.

Destructive or Nondestructive Audio Editing
How you Send an audio file makes a difference.

Destructive audio editing means you are changing the source audio file stored on your hard disk. Nondestructive audio editing means you are not changing the source audio file—either because you are working on a copy of it, or your changes are not permanently attached to the file.

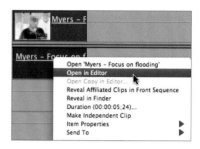

If you Control-click an audio clip and choose **Send to Soundtrack Pro Audio File Project,** you create a duplicate audio file using a name that you supply. When you open that file in Soundtrack Pro, you are doing nondestructive editing because the source clip on your hard disk does not change.

If you Control-click the clip and choose **Open in Editor,** Soundtrack Pro opens the source clip on your hard disk for editing, which makes all your changes destructive.

● **NOTE**

Sending clips to a Soundtrack Pro Multitrack Project only sends pointers to files, which means your audio is edited and mixed non-destructively.

● **NOTE**

Because of its destructive nature, I don't like Soundtrack Pro scripts. Unless you pay close attention to a warning dialog box, it is very easy to destructively edit your source audio. If you make a mistake, you have permanently damaged your source audio and your only option is to recapture the clip.

CHAPTER 7

Transitions and Effects

Let's face it. The fun of editing is in creating transitions and effects. That's not to say the rest of the process is dull and boring, but nothing adds spice and interest to a project like the perfect effect at the perfect time.

The problem is, creating those effects can take *forever*!

In this chapter, you'll learn dozens of techniques you can use to simplify, speed up, or simply supply special sizzle to your sequences. (And I'll try to do it without applying any more awful alliteration.)

It... Just... Won't... Fade...!

Make a clip completely fade to black at the end of a sequence.

Final Cut Pro is a very helpful program. Whenever it sees a gap *between* two clips, it assumes that you want to fill that gap with black. So, it cheerfully—and invisibly—fills any gap with TV-safe video black, audio black, and timecode.

However, the rules that Final Cut follows tell it to fill gaps only when there is a clip on either side of the gap. This is not the case when you reach the end of a sequence. Since this is the last clip, Final Cut doesn't know what to do—so it does nothing; it just parks on the last frame. This means that if you are fading to black, the fade *almost* reaches black... but not quite. There's still a trace of the last image lingering in the Canvas. And it lingers. And it lingers... all because the play-head stops one frame too early.

Here's how to fix this never-ending fade:

1. Put your playhead at the end of the last clip.

2. In the Viewer, open the Generator menu (the icon has the letter A on it) in the lower-right corner of the Video tab and select **Slug**.

3. Change the slug length to anything that seems appropri-ate. For example, if this is video you're laying off to tape, you might set the duration to 60 seconds. If this is a video for the Web, you might use one second.

4. Edit the slug to the Timeline immediately after the transition.

Ta-da! A perfect fade to black.

● NOTE

If you want, you can dissolve between the last clip and the slug. But it isn't necessary. You'll achieve the same effect by simply editing the slug so it's the next clip after the transition. And editing the clip is faster.

● NOTE

Slugs are also a great way to add black leader to the end of your program when you lay it back to tape. I recommend using 60 seconds of black slug.

Apply the Default Audio and Video Transition Simultaneously
Why click twice when you can click once?

Normally, to apply the default video transition, you select the video edit point and press **Command+T**. Then, you select the audio edit point and press **Option+Command+T**.

Great... twice the work to add one transition. However, here's a simple trick for applying both the default video and audio transitions to all selected edit points at the same time:

1. Select the edit point either by Command-clicking each or by drawing the Edit Selection tool (press **G**) around the edit points you want to select.

2. Control-click the edit point and select **Apply Transition "Cross Dissolve"** from the contextual menu.

Two for the price of one!

> **NOTE**
> This trick applies to any selected edit points, including clips that aren't linked or that are on multiple tracks.

Setting the Default Transition
Here's an easy way to modify the default transition.

By default, the standard video transition is a 1-second cross-dissolve and the standard audio transition is a 1-second cross-fade +3 dB. Personally, I like both these transitions, but I don't like either of these durations. For my taste, the video transition is too long and the audio transition is way too long. Here's how to change them—quickly!

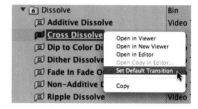

1. Click the **Effects** tab in the Browser to open it.

2. Open the disclosure triangle next to **Video Transitions** and click a triangle to open a bin; for example, the Dissolve bin. The current default transition is underlined.

3. Select the transition you want to make your new default.

4. Change the length, if needed, by scrolling right a few columns in the Browser and double-clicking in the **Length** column for that transition and entering the duration you prefer.

5. Control-click the name of the transition and select **Set Default Transition**, or choose **Effects > Video Transitions > Set Default**.

See how this underlines the name of the transition you chose? This indicates your new default!

● **NOTE**

My favorite video transition is 20 frames. My favorite audio transition is 5 frames. By the way, audio transitions often sound better if their duration is an odd number of frames.

● **EXTRA CREDIT**

The same procedure works for changing the default audio transition, except you set the selected audio transition using **Effects > Audio Transitions > Set Default** instead.

Creating an Alpha Transition
This new effect uses a third video to transition from one shot to the next.

Normally, when you dissolve or wipe from one shot to the next, a total of two video elements are used: the old shot and the new shot.

In Final Cut Pro 7, however, Apple has added a new transition called an Alpha Transition, which can create some cool new effects. (By the way, the term *alpha* simply refers to transparency. Just as the Red channel describes how much red each pixel contains, the Alpha channel describes how transparent each pixel is. Apple could have called it the transparency channel—but they didn't.)

Here's how it works:

1. Select the video edit point.

2. Choose **Effects > Video Transitions > Wipe > Alpha Transition**. The transition is applied to the selected edit point.

3. Double-click the transition icon in the Timeline to load it into the Viewer.

4. The Alpha Transition dialog box appears in the Viewer. The top portion is similar to other transitions. The bottom portion, however, has some new goodies:

   Clip is where you put the video clip that appears as the foreground of the transition. For instance, let's say we have a plane flying through the frame. If the clip only contains the image of the plane, it goes in the top box and you need to add a matte to the second box. If the plane clip contains both the image of the plane and an alpha channel, put the video in the top box and leave the other two boxes empty.

   Clip Alpha Matte is where you put the matte clip containing the alpha channel; that is, the

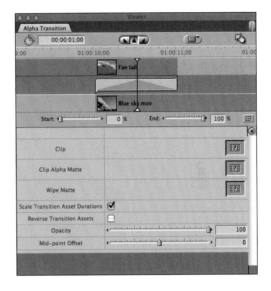

● **EXTRA CREDIT**
The transition between shot 1 and 2 happens in the middle of the transition. If you want it to occur earlier or later, adjust the Mid-point Offset slider

transparency data about the image in the top box. In our example, this contains an alpha channel with the silhouette of the plane matching the movement of the clip in the top box. The silhouette is opaque; the rest of the frame is transparent. Only clips with alpha channels go here.

The **Wipe Matte** clip is used when you have a matte with a silhouette, but not an alpha channel. These were used a lot when effects were recorded to video tape. Most of the time, this box will be left empty.

Creating Custom Transitions You Can Reuse

You can create a custom transition once, then use it over and over again.

In projects where you want to use the same customized transition over and over, here's a fast way to do it. (This tip was first suggested to me by Adam Lloyd Connell.)

Create the transition between two clips in the Timeline and modify it until you are happy. Then, drag the transition icon from the Timeline into the Browser. (You can create an Effects bin to store them in.) Not to worry— the original transition stays put in the Timeline.

Then, whenever you need to use that transition again, just drag it from the Browser to the Timeline.

You could also make the transition a Favorite. However, the problem with Favorites is that everything in the Favorites folder is lost when you trash your Final Cut Pro preferences. By storing the transition in the Browser, you ensure that it's saved with the project and never gets trashed with Preferences.

● **EXTRA CREDIT**

Because you can copy bins from one project to the next, you can easily create a "Favorite transitions" bin in one project, then drag it from the old project to the new project if you need to access the effects.

Applying Multiple Transitions at the Same Time on the Same Track

Introducing a huge new feature in Final Cut Pro 7—with a hidden option.

One of the most requested features from users over the years is the ability to apply multiple transitions at the same time on the same track. With the release of Final Cut Pro 7, that dream has finally become possible.

Here's how it works.

Select the clips to which you want to add a transition. At this point, you can:

- Press **Command+T** to apply the default transition to all selected clips.
- Place your playhead in the middle of the selected clips and apply any audio or video transition from the Effects menu.
- Drag the transition you want to apply from the Effects tab in the Browser.

You'll apply the transition to the beginning and end of every selected clip. Very cool—but only the beginning!

If you don't want the transition at the beginning or end of all the selected clips, set In and Out points. Then transitions are only applied between the In and Out.

NOTE

As with any transition, you need to have handles, extra video, at the ends of all clips to which you want to apply transitions.

EXTRA CREDIT

Put your playhead in the middle of the selected clips and select a new transition from the Effects menu; the new transition replaces the old ones!

EXTRA CREDIT

If you drag a transition and place it on top of just a single transition, it only changes that one transition. However, you can't replace all transitions by dragging a new transition to the selected group of clips.

Selecting Multiple Edit Points on Multiple Tracks
Here's a fast way to select multiple edit points on multiple tracks at the same time.

While you can use the new feature introduced in the previous Power Skill to add multiple transitions, sometimes you just need to select specific edit points, say for some fast trimming. A fast way to select one edit point per track is to use the **Edit Selection** tool.

Press **G**, then drag a rectangular marquee around the edit points you want to select. When you let go, the Trim Edit window opens. You can either adjust your edits in that window, or close the window and adjust them on the Timeline.

I use this technique a lot when I want all the selected edit points to start or end at the same time:

1. Select the edit points you want to move.
2. Put the playhead where you want the edit points to jump.
3. Press **E**.

● **EXTRA CREDIT**
You can also select widely divergent edit points by Command-clicking the edit points you want to select.

Find and Replace Multiple Transitions at Once
This technique can save you a lot of work.

Let's say you've edited a sequence and filled it with transitions. (Christine Steele showed me this tip.)

Let's say that some of these transitions are the same—in this case, I used a combination of Cross-Dissolves and Cube Spins. The transitions are all different lengths and scattered throughout my project.

Then I woke up one morning and realized that all those Cube Spins looked really dated and I needed to change them to something different—say a Fade in Fade Out Dissolve.
This is easy:

1. Open the sequence you want to change in the Timeline.

2. Select **Edit > Find** (or press **Command+F**).

3. Enter **Cube** (or the first portion of the name of the transition you want to replace).

4. Click **Find All**.

   Final Cut Pro selects all the transitions in the Timeline containing that name—something that can't be done any other way.

5. From the Effects menu, select the transition you want to use in place of the selected transition.

   All selected transitions are replaced by the new transition, which also inherit all the old transitions durations and locations.

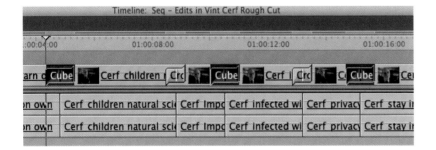

Another Trick for Applying Multiple Transitions at Once
Impress people at parties with this!

This trick is a fast way to apply the default video, or audio, transition to multiple clips at the same time on the same track:

1. Build a sequence in the Timeline (make sure all your clips have handles).

2. Move your playhead to the start of the first clip where you want the transitions to begin.

3. Select all the clips to which you want to add the default transition.

4. Drag all the clips up to the Canvas, and drop them on the red Overwrite with Transition overlay.

5. All your clips are immediately edited back to the Timeline with the default video transition (normally a 30-frame cross-dissolve) applied between each clip.

● NOTE

Unlike the new multiple transition feature of Final Cut Pro 7, this technique can be used by many older versions of Final Cut Pro.

Take a QuickView of Your Effect
The QuickView window is a great way to preview an effect.

While Final Cut continues to get faster with each new version and hardware upgrade, there are times when you are confronted by the dreaded red render bar.

At this point, you have two choices: start rendering, then, while that's processing, return to that 800-page novel you should now have time to finish, or… use the QuickView window.

I opt for QuickView.

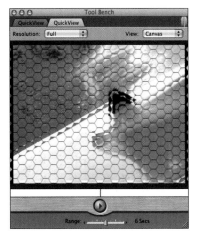

Put your playhead in the middle of the clip that has the effect you want to preview. Select **Tools > QuickView**. A window opens on top of the Viewer. (By the way, if you want the QuickView window to be bigger, a fast way to do that is to make the Viewer bigger before you open QuickView.)

QuickView plays a range of video from the Timeline, ranging from a default of 2 seconds to a maximum of 10. The first time through, it builds a RAM preview. The second, and succeeding, times through, it plays your effect in real time.

● **EXTRA CREDIT**

QuickView centers the current position of the playhead in the window. If the range is set to 5 seconds, it plays 2.5 seconds past the current position of the playhead, then goes back 2.5 seconds before the current position and plays for 5 seconds. Consequently, make sure your playhead is in the middle of what you want to see before opening this window.

Play Unrendered Clips
Of all the keyboard shortcuts in Final Cut Pro, this one is my favorite.

Those dratted red render bars! When your computer is not fast enough to play an effect or transition in real time, Final Cut lets you know by displaying a render bar at the top of the Timeline. Whether the bar is orange or yellow or red, it means that if you want to see your effect perfectly and in real time you need to render.

Of course, you could simply render the effect by choosing **Sequence > Render All** or selecting what you need to render and choosing **Sequence > Render Selection**.

Or…

You could use my absolutely #1 keyboard shortcut: put the playhead at the start of what you want to watch and press **Option+P**. This plays the clip as fast as the computer can calculate the effect, without first rendering the clip. This means that this plays slower than real time.

If you need to see your effect in real time, you need to render. Most of the time, however, you just want to *see* your effect. In which case, Option+P can save you hours on every project!

● **EXTRA CREDIT**

Want to see your video play in Frame Viewer? Press **Option+P**.

● **EXTRA CREDIT**

Want to see if your white levels are OK? Choose **View > Range Check > Excess Luma** and press **Option+P**.

● **EXTRA CREDIT**

Want to see almost anything that doesn't play in real time? Press **Option+P**.

Replace a Clip Without Losing Its Effects
You can add effects to a clip; why not add a clip to an effect?

Generally, when you copy and paste a clip, you want to copy everything associated with that clip—the video image, audio, timecode, as well as any filters and motion effects.

However, sometimes you might want to keep the effects but replace the content of the clip. I ran into this a while ago when I was using freeze frames as transitions between segments. The producer loved the effect—sort of a morphing posterization combined with a text type-on—but naturally he wanted to change the images I was using as the freeze frame.

Here's how to do it:

1. Select the clip containing the new video.

2. Select **Edit > Copy** (or press **Command+C**) to copy it to the clipboard.

3. Select the clip that has the content you want to replace.

4. Select **Edit > Paste Attributes** (or press **Option+V**).

5. Deselect all options except **Content**.

6. Click **OK**.

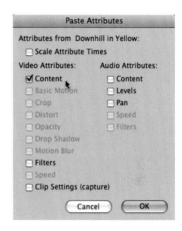

● **NOTE**

Paste Attributes is an excellent tool when you want to replace some effects attached to a clip, but not everything.

● **NOTE**

Paste Attributes does not work with any settings that you create or adjust using the Controls tab of the Viewer.

Invisibility Doesn't Take a Cloak

Green visibility lights are not the best way to make a single clip invisible.

The green visibility lights for each track in Final Cut Pro are useful when you want to toggle a track off or on. However, whenever you change the visibility light for a track, *all* render files associated with that track are deleted. This could be a problem.

While you can use Undo after changing the status of a track, that assumes you made no changes since you changed the track status. Here's an often better option:

For video, if you want to make a clip invisible so that you can see what's below it, Control-click the clip and turn off **Clip Enable**. You still lose render files, but only those files associated with that clip, and not the entire track. (The shortcut is **Control+B**.)

To make a clip visible, repeat the same process—Clip Enable is a toggle.

● **NOTE**

The green visibility lights control more than just track visibility. When a green light is off, clips on that track do not display on the Timeline, nor do they render, output to tape, or export.

● **NOTE**

Whenever you change the visibility of a track, you always lose your render files. (Yes, Final Cut will warn you.) This is because render files are associated with the sequence, not the clip, and since you are changing what's visible in the sequence, the render files need to change.

ProRes Enlarges Its Family

Apple increases the ProRes count to five.

All video is encoded using a codec. DV, HDV, XDCAM, and HDCAM are all examples of video codecs. A codec is neither good nor bad—it's a necessary part of the digital video process.

In the past, codecs have been specific to particular cameras, or formats. With the release of Final Cut Studio 2, Apple introduced a new family of codecs that were not tied to a particular format. Instead, they allowed different—and often incompatible—video formats to be converted into a high-quality common format.

With the release of the latest version of Final Cut Studio, Apple increased the number of ProRes codecs to five, as shown in the following table.

PRORES CODECS IN FINAL CUT PRO 7

Version	Data Rate	To Store One Hour of HD
ProRes 422 Proxy	5.6 MB/s	20 GB
ProRes 422 LT	12.75 MB/s	46 GB
ProRes 422	18.1 MB/s	66 GB
ProRes 422 HQ	27.5 MB/s	99 GB
ProRes 4444 ("ProRes 4x4")	41.25 MB/s	148 GB (does not include alpha channel)

All five of these flavors share the same characteristics. They all:

- Compress their images using I-frames, which is better than GOP compression
- Use 10 bits to define their pixels, which is better than 8-bit video found in DV or HDV
- Use variable bit-rate compression, to keep file size down
- Offer a very high image quality

Only the ProRes 4444 version provides alpha channels, which means it can retain the transparency information in a clip. The rest do not.

If you are working with a single video format, ProRes may not be that helpful. But as you start to mix and match between formats, ProRes should definitely be part of your workflow.

Change Codecs to Improve Render Quality and Speed
Changing codecs is important if you are working in HDV, XDCAM HD, or XDCAM EX.

Normally, it's easier to render your effects and transitions using the same video format you're editing. In other words, your render format should match your sequence settings. However, for some video formats—for example, those that use a GOP compression scheme—changing render settings can improve quality and allow renders to be completed faster.

To change your render settings, choose **Sequence > Settings** and select the **Render Control** tab. Then, change the Codec pop-up menu to **Apple ProRes 422**. Render times should speed up over 40 percent!

The one disadvantage to this technique is that your file sizes will be about four times larger than the native format. However, you may decide that the performance gains outweigh this.

> **NOTE**
> Video formats this works for include all varieties of HDV, XDCAM HD, and XDCAM EX. Formats like AVCHD, though GOP-compressed, are converted to ProRes automatically during ingest, so they won't benefit from this technique.

> **NOTE**
> In my testing, changing the codec has no impact on output or export speed, but will increase render speeds up to 40 percent. Also, ProRes should provide higher-quality effects and transitions.

> **EXTRA CREDIT**
> You can make this a permanent setting for all future projects by choosing **Final Cut Pro > User Preferences > Render Control**. This changes the render settings for all future sequences that you create.

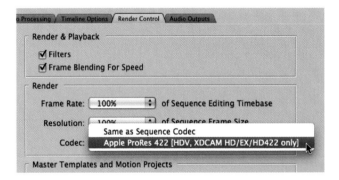

Render Your Sequences Automatically
Auto-Render saves you more time than you might expect.

Wouldn't it be nice if Final Cut Pro could do its rendering "in the background," while you're working in Photoshop, checking your e-mail, or updating your accounting? It can and here's how.

Auto-Render is essentially a timer that tells Final Cut Pro to do something when it isn't busy. And that's the key word: *busy*. Final Cut Pro considers itself not busy when there are no mouse clicks or key presses. That means whenever Final Cut Pro is running in the background, it is suddenly "not busy."

To set this feature, choose **Final Cut Pro > User Preferences** and click the **General** tab. In the lower-right corner is Auto-Render. I consider the default setting of 45 to be too long and change it to **15**. This means that Auto-Render kicks in after 15 minutes of inactivity.

Here's the secret: when you switch to another application, keep Final Cut Pro open. Since Final Cut Pro doesn't see any mouse or keyboard activity, it figures it isn't busy, so after 15 minutes it renders all open sequences, even though you're busy working in another application.

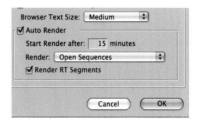

NOTE

Auto-Render has no effect when you are running Final Cut Pro—only when you are using other programs and Final Cut Pro is running in the background.

Render All Doesn't

The default settings of Render All actually miss things.

According to Apple, in the default setting, when you render using **Sequence > Render All**, the **Full** option (shown here) is not enabled. This category refers to sequence items with real-time effects that are capable of playback and output to video at full quality with no rendering required. There may be differences in the Canvas display between real-time playback and fully rendered material.

To ensure a consistent playback quality in the Canvas, enable (check) the Full Render category before rendering.

● **EXTRA CREDIT**

Also, make a point to check *every* line item when you choose **Sequence > Render Selection**; otherwise, that option skips stuff as well. These options remain checked until you trash your Final Cut Pro preferences.

Make the FrameViewer Move
The FrameViewer just shows stills—unless you know this secret.

The FrameViewer (**Tools > FrameViewer**, or press **Option+7**) allows you to compare two different shots in the same window—such as the current frame with and without filters, or the current and previous shot. The problem is that when you play your sequence, the FrameViewer does not update. Unless, as Duke Bishop suggested recently, you fool it into playing.

When FrameViewer is open, the current frame will update when you use the Left/Right Arrow keys, drag with the playhead, or press **Option+P**.

I love tricks like this!

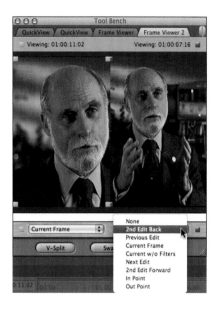

● **NOTE**

In case you were wondering, the previous or next edit frame doesn't update because the FrameViewer is showing the Out or In point of that clip, which doesn't change as you move the playhead.

Viewing Clips on Different Tracks
Here's a great way to compare clips stacked vertically but widely separated by tracks.

Most of the time, our projects have only a few tracks and we can easily see and compare clips within the Timeline. But, sometimes our video effects or audio tracks start stacking clips like floors in a skyscraper and it becomes impossible to see all the clips at once. Worse, if we need to align a clip on a high track with a clip on a lower track, things get tricky—unless you know this next technique.

Running horizontally through the center of the Timeline is a double gray bar. While we generally consider this the separator between audio and video, it actually has a deeper function.

Go to the right side of the Timeline and drag one of the rounded thumbs up, to surround the lower video tracks, or down, surrounding the lower audio tracks. This draws a heavy gray rectangle around the lower tracks— in this example, I'm capturing V1 and V2.

Now, grab the thumb in the middle and drag it up (for video) or down (for audio) and notice how you can compare the timing of the clips in the boxed area with those on higher tracks. Since Final Cut Pro allows up to 99 tracks of video or audio, this can be a useful technique when your tracks are widely separated vertically.

● **EXTRA CREDIT**

Once you have captured a track, you can change the size of the captured area by dragging either the top or bottom gray edge with the mouse.

To gain more room to view audio or video clips, when the double gray bar is collapsed, forming a thick gray bar, simply drag the bar up or down in the Timeline.

A Fast Way to Find Effects
You can tell in a snap whether a clip has any effects on it.

Ever want to know if a clip in the Timeline has any effects applied to it? Press **Option+T** to toggle **Clip Keyframes** on. (It's the button with green and blue stripes in the lower-left corner of the Timeline.)

Any clip with a *green* line under it has a filter applied. Any clip with a *blue* line under it has a motion effect applied. For example, in this illustration, the first clip has a motion effect, the second has a filter effect, and the third has both a filter and motion effect.

● **NOTE**
This button also allows you to edit motion and filter effects, and their associated keyframes, in the Timeline, which is worth its own Power Skill a bit later.

● **EXTRA CREDIT**
This button displays a lot of information hidden in the Timeline. To restrict what is displayed, Control-click the clip and only check the settings you want to see.

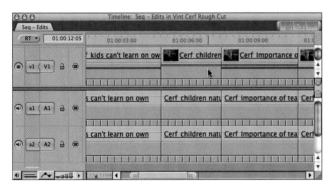

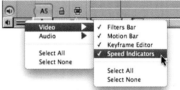

Finding an Effect in the Browser
Find effects as fast as you find a clip!

If you only have a few effects, this technique isn't that useful. But as you start to accumulate more and more third-party filters, transitions, generators, and other toys, this Power Skill can help you avoid hours spent searching for an effect.

Because the Browser is a database, you can use **Edit > Find** to locate clips. You can also do the same with Effects. Click the Effects tab in the Browser to make it active, choose **Edit > Find** (or press **Command+F**), and enter the name, or a portion of the name, of the effect you want to find in the lower-right text box.

Then, click **Find** to find the first effect that meets your criteria, or **Find All** to display all the effects that match your search.

● **EXTRA CREDIT**
Click the More button to reveal additional search criteria. In this example, I am searching for all effects that start with the word "Cross" but exclude "Dissolve."

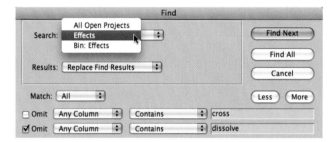

Creating a Favorite
Playing favorites is easy...

Final Cut creates favorite effects and favorite motions and stores them in the Favorites folder in the Effects tab in the Browser. Favorite effects are created from the Filters tab, while favorite motions are created from the Motion tab.

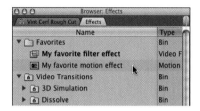

Here's how to create a favorite Filter effect:

1. Apply and modify a filter, or group of filters, to a clip.

2. Make sure the clip is loaded into the Viewer and that the Viewer window is active.

3. Select the Filter tab, and then choose **Effects > Make Favorite Effect** (or press **Option+F**).

And here's how to create a favorite Motion effect:

1. Load a clip into the Viewer and modify the settings on the Motion tab.

2. Make sure the Viewer is selected.

2. Select the Motion tab, and then choose **Effects > Make Favorite Motion** (or press **Control+F**).

You can create an unlimited number of favorites and rename them in the Effects tab. The first five effects in each category are automatically assigned keyboard shortcuts.

● **NOTE**
You can't create a single favorite that includes both filters and motions in one favorite.

● **NOTE**
You can't create favorites from settings in the Controls tab.

● **NOTE**
A group of filters is called a filter stack. Be careful not to open that filter folder in the Effects tab, as this changes the order of the clips.

Save Your Favorites

Favorites can be trashed accidentally—here's how to save them.

The good thing about favorites is that you can create them easily and reuse them between projects. The bad thing is that they are stored in your preference files, so when you trash preferences, your favorites get trashed as well.

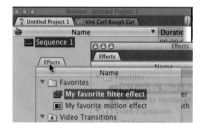

It's time for a workaround.

To keep your favorites permanently, assuming that you have already created a variety of favorite effects, follow these steps:

1. Create a new project.

2. Tear the **Effects** tab away from the Browser tab so you can see the contents of both the project and effects tabs.

3. Drag your entire **Favorites** folder from the Effects tab into the Browser tab.

4. Save the file. Effects stored in the Browser of a project file are not affected when you trash preferences.

To restore filters from this project folder, drag the *contents* of the Favorites folder in your Browser into your Favorites folder in your Effects tab. Dragging the contents means you won't accidentally replace any new favorites you may have created.

● **NOTE**

While effects in the Browser won't appear in your Favorites menu, you can apply any effect in the Browser by simply dragging it from the Browser onto a clip.

● **NOTE**

You can't assign keyboard shortcuts to effects stored in the Browser.

● **EXTRA CREDIT**

Instead of creating a favorite, drag your filter, motion effect, or transition directly from the Timeline into the Browser (you can put them in bins so you'll know what you've stored where).

Using Motion Templates
Harness the graphics power of Motion without knowing anything about Motion.

Motion is a great program. However, for a variety of reasons editors are often afraid to use it. For that reason, Apple invented Motion templates. Motion templates allow you to add high-quality motion graphics to your Final Cut Pro projects without understanding anything about motion graphics.

You can see what I'm talking about by choosing **Sequence > Add Master Template**. These templates can be accessed from a variety of menus in Final Cut, but you need to be careful what you select before you open the template menu.

If the Timeline is selected when you access this menu, the buttons in the bottom right say Superimpose, Overwrite, and Insert, which allow you to edit the template directly into the Timeline.

If, on the other hand, you select the Browser, Viewer, or Canvas before opening the template window, the lower-right corner only contains one button, Open, which opens the template into the Viewer.

● **NOTE**

Superimpose decides where to locate the template based on the location of the playhead. Superimpose places the template on the track above the track containing the v1 patch (on the left of the Timeline), trimmed to the same length and location as the clip your playhead is in.

● **EXTRA CREDIT**

You can open Motion templates by opening the Browser and clicking the Effects tab, by choosing from the Effects menu, or by Control-clicking a clip in the Timeline. But my choice is **Sequence > Add Master Template**, because that's the only option that allows me to see the template before applying it.

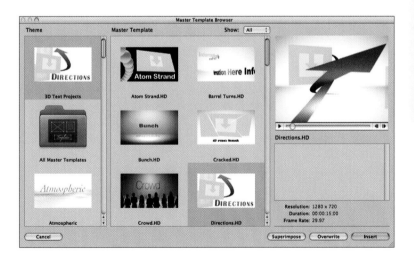

Replace Templates with Blinding Speed
Oops—added the wrong Motion template to your sequence? Replace it fast!

One of the very cool, but hidden, tricks of Motion templates is that replacing any of the following is easy:

- A single occurrence of a template in a sequence
- Every occurrence of that template in a single sequence
- Every occurrence of that template in every sequence in that project

The reason this is so cool is that when you replace the template, all the text, images, timings, and locations remain the same. Only the template changes. However, to use this, you need to be patient:

1. Open into the Timeline the sequence containing the template(s) you want to replace.

2. Select the Viewer and choose **Sequence > Add Master Template**.

3. Open the new Motion template you want to use in the Viewer. This is important—the template needs to be in the Viewer.

4. Grab the template in the Viewer and drag it on top of the template you want to replace in the Timeline. Then, wait…

After a few seconds a menu pops up allowing you to replace *just* the template you're dragging the new version on, or *every* instance of this template in your sequence, or every instance of this template in the *entire* project.

● **NOTE**

This is a good way to use a Motion template as a placeholder. Pick a template to use while the graphics artist is creating the template you want. Then, virtually instantly, you can replace all the temporary graphics with the final graphics while retaining all the text, images, and timing of the original templates.

Where Motion Templates Are Stored

To use Motion templates across a network, you need to change where they're stored.

By default, custom Motion templates are stored in the Home directory of the computer that installed the Motion application. (The specific route is: **Home Directory > Library > Application Support > Final Cut Studio > Motion > Templates**.)

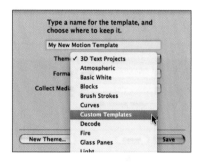

For single-user systems, while this location is OK, I make a point to store all my Final Cut Studio data to a second drive, so that I don't take up space on my boot drive.

However, in a network situation, these templates could not be stored in a worse place. There is no way for another user to get access to your home directory. To solve this problem, reinstall your Motion data files to a folder on a shared network drive. This resets the pointers in both Motion and Final Cut Pro showing where your Motion templates are stored.

However, this next step is critical. Create folders (Apple calls them Themes) in this network template folder *before* you save any templates. If a custom folder is created before saving the file, Motion stores the new template to the network location. If a folder is not created, Motion creates a new Theme folder and stores the new template in the home directory of the computer that saved the Motion file.

Matching Fonts Between Motion and Final Cut Pro

Text created in Motion doesn't match the same text in Final Cut Pro—here's why.

If you've used a font and point size in Motion, then moved that file into Final Cut Pro and tried to match the font, you've found they don't match. While Motion and Final Cut Pro calculate the font *size* the same, they don't calculate font *tracking* the same. The following screenshot illustrates the problem.

To match fonts between the two applications, make sure to use the same font and point size in both applications. Then, to get them to match, open the Final Cut text clip in the Controls tab in the Viewer and adjust the **Center**, **Tracking**, and **Leading** settings.

● **NOTE**

While specific numbers will vary by font and size, setting Center to **2, −50**, Tracking from **1.6** to **1.8**, and Leading from **0** to **−4** should get your text to match.

Sharing Motion Projects
Motion doesn't make moving project files easy.

Matt Davis sent me this tip.

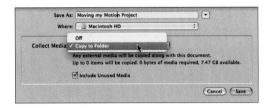

When moving a Motion project between computers, you can't simply move the Motion project as it won't contain any movies, images, or sounds that you've added to the project. Motion just points to your assets—it doesn't contain them.

So, to move a Motion project to another machine, choose **File > Save As**, enter your desired name, and select **Copy to Folder** from the Collect Media pop-up menu. This trick stores all the assets used in your Motion project in one convenient place.

In the process, Motion tells you how much space the assets will take, and places them in a subfolder called **Media** in the same location as your Motion project. Depending upon the assets you are using, this may become quite a large folder!

Once this folder is on the client's system, all you need to do is to email the Motion project to the client and tell them to put it in the same

> **NOTE**
> Motion sometimes has problems sending custom font information using this process. In that case, send your client a QuickTime movie of your project using **File > Export > QuickTime Movie** from Final Cut Pro.

folder. That way, by using the same folder on both systems, Motion's links to the media will be maintained.

If you add any new elements to your project, be sure to send them to the client with instructions to place it in the Media folder for this project.

What Is a Wireframe?
And why would you use it?

A wireframe displays the outline of your clip. Although you can't see the image it contains, you can see where the image is located, its shape, and where it moves through the frame.

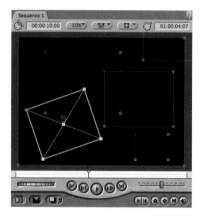

The benefit of a wireframe is that no matter how complex your motion effect, wireframes never need rendering; you can always watch them in real time. If you have a ton of clips all moving around the frame, this is a great way to check their movements without needing to render every time you make a change.

To switch to Wireframe mode, select either the Canvas or Viewer, and then select **View > Wireframe**; select **Wireframe** from the rightmost pop-up menu at the top of the Viewer or Canvas; or select the window you want to switch to Wireframe mode and press **W** twice.

• NOTE

Wireframe mode is not the same as pressing the Caps Lock key. When the Caps Lock key is on, all rendering is stopped. This is a holdover from when computers were much slower and it could take 30 seconds just to display a frame after you applied a Blur. By pressing the Caps Lock key, you'd see your frame immediately, but not the effect applied to it.

Title Safe, Action Safe, and the New SD Boundaries
New boundaries allow you to shoot 16:9 and protect 4:3.

Title Safe and Action Safe are guides that allow camera operators and effects composi- tors to make sure that all essential elements of their images can be seen by most viewers.

These grew out of the vagaries of analog television sets, but continue into the digital age as much of our material is still down- converted to older analog TV sets. Also, we still have issues with image cropping on HD rear-projection screens and digital theater projection.

To compensate for this, we draw a rectangle around our image 5 percent in from all edges—this is called Action Safe. All essential action should be contained inside this outer rectangle; for instance, notice that the danc- er's hands and feet extend right to the line.

Then, 10 percent in from all edges, we draw a second rectangle—this is called Title Safe. All essential text must be contained inside this inner rectangle.

New with the latest version of Final Cut Pro are four short vertical lines. These indicate the boundaries of Action and Title Safe for 4:3 images when shooting 16:9. My camera friends call this "shooting 16:9 but protecting 4:3." This allows you to be sure that all essen- tial elements are inside the 4:3 boundary.

● NOTE

To display these boundary lines, choose **View > Show Title Safe**. If they don't appear, be sure **View > Show Overlays** is also selected.

Quickly Create Text Clips
One keystroke—one text clip. Easy!

Here's a keyboard shortcut that lets you avoid scrolling through several drop-down menus just to create a text clip:

Press **Control+X**.

In an instant a new text clip is loaded into the Viewer. Click the **Controls** tab and start making changes!

● **NOTE**

There is no way to change the default font. It is always Lucida Grande, 36 point, aligned Center.

● **EXTRA CREDIT**

By default, this shortcut creates a 10-second full-screen text clip in the Viewer, matching the video format settings in Easy Setup. Simply alter the duration time in the top-left timecode box of the Video tab to change the length.

Three Steps to Better Text
Here's a fast, three-step process to creating text clips in Final Cut Pro.

Just because you can create a text clip quickly doesn't mean you are done. In fact, many editors create a text clip and start making changes, only to discover that their changes don't show up in the Timeline.

To solve this problem, here's a three-step way to create text in Final Cut that never gets lost. I call it the "Three-Step Text Process." Start by putting your playhead in the middle of the clip you want to superimpose the new text over. Then follow these steps:

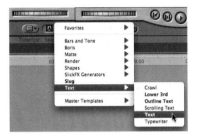

1. Press **Control+X** (or open the Generator menu in the lower-right corner of the Video tab in the Viewer and select **Text > Text**).
2. Drag the clip from the Viewer to the Canvas. An Overlay menu appears; drop the clip on **Superimpose**. This edits the clip to the Timeline, matching the duration of the clip your playhead is in and putting it one track higher than the current position of the v1 patch tab.
3. Double-click the text clip in the Timeline to load it into the Viewer so you can make changes.

Generate—Superimpose—Double-click. Done.

● **EXTRA CREDIT**
If you aren't superimposing the text over a clip, drop the text clip on Overwrite in the Canvas Overlay menu. All text has a default duration of 10 seconds.

Scaling Text in Controls vs. Motion Tab
If you have the choice, always scale your text in the Controls tab.

The difference between scaling a Final Cut text clip in the Controls tab versus the Motion tab is all about quality and flexibility. (Scaling in the Motion tab is the same as scaling directly in the Canvas by dragging wireframes.)

As the left side of the screenshot illustrates, when you scale text in the Controls tab, you are changing the text itself. All text in Final Cut Pro is a mathematical equation, called a vector, that allows text to scale to any size perfectly. The Controls tab takes advantage of this fact.

When you scale text in the Motion tab, you are scaling the frame that *contains* the text. As the right side of the screenshot illustrates, you aren't improving the resolution but are simply blowing up the original image. This causes fuzzy edges, color fringing where different colors meet, and a general softness and lack of quality.

● **EXTRA CREDIT**

When positioning text, use the Controls tab, because that moves the text itself. Positioning text using the Motion tab moves the frame that contains the text. If the edge of a letter is outside the frame, the Controls tab will reveal it; the Motion tab won't.

● **NOTE**

The accompanying image was created using 600-point Curlz positioned and scaled first in the Controls tab, and then repositioned and scaled in the Motion tab.

Drop Shadow Settings

Text needs a drop shadow to make it readable. Here are my favorite drop shadow settings.

We all get excited about the high image quality inherent in high-definition video. However, even 1080p video is barely two megapixels in resolution. For video, this is great. For a still image, it's not worth mentioning in polite company. Standard def (SD), of course, is far, far worse.

All this means that we need to add drop shadows whenever we want people to read the text we display onscreen, especially if the color of the text comes close to matching the color of the background.

To apply a drop shadow:

1. Double-click your text clip to load it into the Viewer and open the **Motion** tab.
2. Check the **Drop Shadow** check box to turn it on.
3. Click the Disclosure triangle to open the dialog box.
4. For HD text, set the Offset to **2.5** (for SD text, use **1.5**).
5. Set Softness to **30**.
6. Set Opacity to **90**.

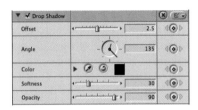

● **EXTRA CREDIT**

To copy the drop shadow settings from one clip to others, select the clip with the settings you like. Choose **Edit > Copy**. Select the clip, or clips, to which you want to transfer the settings. Select **Edit > Paste Attributes**, check only **Drop Shadow**, and then click **OK**.

Constant-Speed Changes in Final Cut Pro 7
We could always change clip speed. Final Cut Pro 7 makes it easier.

Final Cut has two ways to change the speed of a clip: constant and variable. A constant-speed change alters the speed of the entire clip by the same amount. A variable-speed change varies the speed of a clip during playback.

Until recently, making a constant-speed change to a clip always altered the duration of the clip. With the latest release, that's no longer true.

1. Select the clip for which you want to change the speed.

2. Choose **Modify > Change Speed** (or press **Command+J**).

3. You can either enter the actual Duration for the clip in the top-left text box, or enter the percentage change in the Rate text box (top-right corner). The Rate box is faster; the Duration box is more precise.

4. If **Ripple Sequence** is checked, the entire clip will play at the new speed, its duration will change accordingly, and all downstream clips will be adjusted for the new duration of the clip. If **Ripple Sequence** is not checked, the clip will start at the current In point until the current duration of the clip is reached. This means that if the clip is slowed down, not all of the original frames will play. Or, if the clip is sped up, more than the original frames will play back.

EXTRA CREDIT

If you want a clip to run full speed in reverse, click the Reverse check box and leave Rate at **100%**.

NOTE

Constant-speed changes apply to both audio and video.

NOTE

The Start and End curves are for variable-speed changes. You can turn them on for constant-speed changes, but they may create unexpected speed change effects.

Variable-Speed Changes in Final Cut Pro 7
Making variable-speed changes is a lot easier.

In the latest version of Final Cut Pro, Apple changed how variable-speed changes are created. A variable-speed change is where the speed of the clip changes during playback.

There are several ways to create a variable-speed change. Here's one I like:

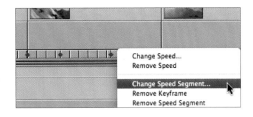

1. In the Tool palette, select the Speed tool (press **SSS**). It looks like a stopwatch in a box. It's in the fifth row from the top of the Tool palette, and is the third one from the left.

2. Display the time keyframe section of the Timeline by pressing **Option+T**, or by clicking the **Toggle Clip Keyframes** button in the lower left of the Timeline (the button has blue and green bars on it).

3. With the Speed tool, click the hash marks at the bottom of a clip to set a keyframe in your timeline clip at the point that you want the speed change to begin.

4. Again, with the Speed tool, set a second keyframe where you want the speed change to either end or change again.

5. Control-click the small blue keyframe at the bottom of the clip in the Timeline graph and select **Change Speed Segment**. This allows you to change the speed just from the previous keyframe to the current one.

> **NOTE**
> Control-clicking a speed keyframe offers a variety of new settings Final Cut Pro hasn't offered before, including the ability to set Ease in and Ease out speeds using the menu.

6. In the Speed dialog box, set **Rate** to the new speed of that segment. Experiment with the **Ease In** and **Ease Out** buttons to change the transition speed into and out of the new segment.

This is a powerful new tool in Final Cut Pro, with more settings than can be covered in one Power Skill. However, the key new changes are to use the Speed tool to set keyframes in the clip in the Timeline, then Control-click the keyframe to select Change Speed Segment.

Apply Multiple Keyframes to Multiple Clips Fast

Without even opening the Viewer, you can add Motion tab keyframes all at once.

Let's say you have a stack of clips in the Timeline that you want to start scaling and rotating all at the same time. Here's a fast way to set motion keyframes in multiple clips at the same time.

1. In the Timeline, put your playhead where you want the keyframes to be placed and select the clips to which you want to apply the keyframes. All the clips you want to add keyframes to must be positioned under the playhead.

2. In the lower-right corner of the Canvas, click the **Add Motion Keyframe** button; it's the one that looks like a diamond.

When you load a clip into the Viewer, notice that keyframes have been added to Scale, Rotation, Center, Anchor Point, Crop, Distort, and Aspect Ratio. The good news is that this sets every Motion tab parameter keyframe at once at the position of the playhead. The bad news is that this sets *every* Motion tab parameter keyframe at once at the position of the playhead.

So, here's the part that makes this technique worthwhile:

Control-click the **Add Keyframes** button and uncheck all the keyframes that you don't want to set when you click this button. Now, you set just the keyframes you want, with a single click of the mouse.

● **NOTE**

This technique does not set keyframes in the Controls or Filter tabs or other Motion tab parameters such as Opacity, Drop Shadow, Motion Blur, or Speed.

● **NOTE**

Once you set a keyframe for a parameter when you reposition the playhead and change the parameter setting, Final Cut Pro sets a new keyframe. This means, generally, you only need to set an opening keyframe, and then just make adjustments thereafter. Final Cut Pro sets the keyframes for you automatically.

Displaying Motion and Filter Keyframes in the Timeline
You can reveal hidden effect keyframes in the Timeline, if you know where to look.

In the lower-left corner of the Timeline is a button with two bars, one green and one blue. Click the **Toggle Clip Keyframes** button to turn on the Timeline keyframe display.

All the tracks are separated by a gray area, and some clips have blue or green bars underneath them.

A green bar under a clip indicates that a filter is applied to the clip.

A blue bar under a clip indicates that a motion effect is applied to the clip.

Small diamonds in a blue or green bar indicate keyframes are applied to the effect.

The small boxes at the bottom of this new gray area indicate the speed of a clip. The width of the boxes changes as the speed of the clip changes.

● **EXTRA CREDIT**

If you need more room to see, right next to the left edge of the track— between the track and the Auto-Select button—is a very thin vertical column. Drag inside this column and you'll expand, or contract, the height of this gray area.

● **EXTRA CREDIT**

To reset all tracks back to their normal height, click one of the four "bar charts" at the bottom left of the Timeline.

Adjusting Effect Keyframes in the Timeline
Not only can you display keyframes in the Timeline, but you can change them there, too!

Say you've applied a Gaussian Blur filter and two motion effects to a clip. Display Timeline keyframes by pressing **Option+T**. The green bar indicates a filter is applied; the diamonds indicate there are keyframes attached to the filter.

Control-click in the gray area under a clip and the pop-up menu displays all the filters applied to the clip (above the thin gray line), and all the available Motion settings.

Select the keyframes you want to change—for this example, choose the Blur keyframes—and a second line shows up at the bottom. This new line contains the Scale keyframes applied to this clip. Filters are displayed as a green line, motion effects use blue lines.

You can now change keyframes in the Timeline, without first loading the clip into the Viewer.

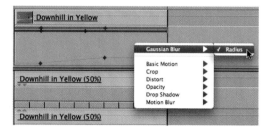

● **NOTE**

I'm of two minds about this feature. It is much faster, but when you load a clip into the Viewer, you can change more than one parameter at a time, whereas here you need to change each parameter individually.

Tossing Keyframes
Keyframes aren't permanent—you can just toss them away. Here's how.

Did you know that you can delete a keyframe in the Timeline by dragging it vertically out of the clip with the mouse?

Grab the keyframe, drag it outside the border of the clip, and watch as the mouse icon changes to a tiny trash can. This works best if you drag quickly.

Release the mouse and your keyframe is no more.

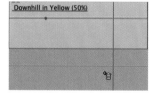

● **NOTE**

This trick also works in the Viewer, but not for Rotation in the Motion tab.

Slipping Keyframes in the Timeline
Here's a fast way to change the timing of keyframes in the Timeline.

Moving all the filter keyframes—or all the motion keyframes attached to a clip—all at once is something we can't do in the Viewer.

Instead, we do it in the Timeline:

1. In the lower-left corner, click the Toggle Clip Keyframes button (or press **Option+T**). As mentioned earlier, clips with blue lines have motion effects applied, and clips with green lines have filter effects applied.

2. Keyframes, if they exist, are indicated by small diamonds in either the green or blue line.

3. Using the Arrow tool, grab the blue line between the diamonds (or the green line—it works the same) and drag it back and forth to slide your keyframe(s) earlier or later in the Timeline, all without going up to the Viewer!

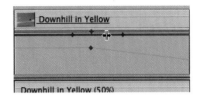

● **EXTRA CREDIT**
If you have lots of keyframed parameters, Control-click the Toggle Clip Keyframes button, and check only the parameter whose keyframes you want to move.

Sliding Keyframes in the Viewer
Here's yet another cool way to move effect keyframes, this time in the Viewer.

Have you ever wanted to move keyframes for an effect? Well, you can, if you have the right tool.

In this example, I've created some keyframes for a motion effect. (This happens to be for scaling, but it works for any keyframed parameter in either the Viewer or the Canvas.)

In the Tool palette, select the **Slip** tool (or press **S**).

Click and drag on the parameter line between the two keyframes and they all change position.

● **NOTE**
This technique shifts *all* the keyframes associated with that parameter. You can't select just a group of keyframes and move them.

● **NOTE**
This technique won't work if any of the keyframes are positioned on the first or last frame of a clip.

Creating Moves on Still Images
Getting movement within still images is tricky—but less so after you read this.

Looking for a quick way to create movement on still images (known as the "Ken Burns effect"), but don't want the hassle of creating keyframes in Motion?

Here's one solution, suggested by Eric Cosh and John Kaplan:

1. Open your stills in iPhoto and make a separate album (folder) in iPhoto called **image montage** (or whatever name suits your fancy) containing only the shots you want to move in it.

2. Click the **Slideshow** icon at the bottom of the iPhoto window. Choose **Ken Burns Effect** with a dissolve duration of one second or faster.

3. Choose **File > Export > As a File** and export it as a QuickTime movie.

4. Import the new QuickTime file into Final Cut Pro, edit it to your sequence, and render.

● **EXTRA CREDIT**

When creating this effect in iPhoto, you may notice that the motion is randomly applied, in both direction and location on picture. Although you cannot control the type of motion, you can drag the picture to set where the motioning will end. You're essentially setting the key focal point. This is a handy tip when iPhoto decides to pan down to a crotch rather than up to a face.

● **NOTE**

Another program that makes moves on stills very easy is PhotoMotion from GeeThree (www.geethree. com). It works as a Final Cut Pro plug-in.

Fun with the Anchor Point

The anchor point controls more than rotation. Check this out and see.

Have you ever wondered what the anchor point does in the Motion tab? Well, let's find out:

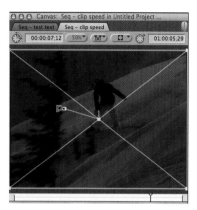

1. Load an image you want to manipulate from the Timeline into the Viewer.

2. Select the Canvas, and choose **Image + Wireframe** either from the View menu or the small pop-up menu at the top right of the Canvas. The white dot that appears connected to the center of your image is the anchor point.

3. Select the **Distort** tool (press **D**), and then drag the point to move it. You could also enter the coordinates for the anchor point directly in the Viewer, if you want to be precise about it.

Now for some fun. Select the **Motion** tab in the Viewer and watch what happens in the Canvas when you do the following:

- Rotate your image—it rotates around the anchor point.

- Drag the Scale slider—it scales from its original position and gradually recedes into the anchor point.

> ● **NOTE**
>
> Moving the anchor point to a corner of the image is an interesting way to have an image scale and reposition automatically.

Create a Filter Range
You can apply filters to only a portion of a clip—without cutting the clip.

You can limit the range of a filter in two ways: before or after you apply a filter. This can save you having to create keyframes for something simple like blurring a logo.

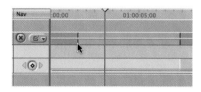

To create a range within a clip *before* you apply a filter, from the Tool palette select the **Range Selection** tool (or press **G** three times). Then, drag across the portion of the clip to which you want to apply the filter. When you apply a filter, it will only apply to the selected portion of the clip, or clips.

To create a range within a clip *after* the filter has been applied, double-click a clip to load it into the Viewer and click the Filter tab.

If you look closely at the top of the filter bar, you'll see a dark black vertical bar at the beginning and end of the clip; the bar at the beginning is often hard to see. Grab and drag each of these two heavy black vertical lines at the top of the filter to alter the range of the clip to which the filter applies.

● **NOTE**

When you use the Range Selection tool, these black bars are moved automatically by the tool to create the range.

● **NOTE**

A clip range can extend across multiple clips.

● **EXTRA CREDIT**

Put the Arrow tool between these two black bars and you can slip the range within the clip. This won't work if the bars are at the beginning and end of the clip; filter ranges need to have handles, like clips, in order for slipping to work.

A Fast Way to Remove Filters
This tip makes removing filters from a range of clips a snap.

Select all the clips from which you want to remove the filters. Choose **Edit > Remove Attributes**, check **Filters** (leave all the other settings unchecked), and click **OK**. This removes *all* the filters from the selected clip(s). Using this technique, you can't remove just some of the filters assigned to a clip, you either remove all of them or none.

But if all the selected clips have the same set of filters, you *can* remove selected filters and keep the others. To do this, we'll create a model clip, and then copy the settings from that model to the other clips.

1. Open a clip to the Viewer and select the **Filters** tab.

2. Remove the filter(s) you want to get rid of by highlighting the name of the filter and pressing **Delete**.

3. Highlight the clip with the new set of filters in the Timeline and select **Edit > Copy** (or press **Command+C**).

4. Highlight all the clips in the Timeline that you want to change and select **Edit > Remove Attributes**, check only the **Filters** check box, and click **OK**.

5. Keep those same clips selected. Go to **Edit > Paste Attributes** (or press **Option+V**), check only the **Filters** check box, and click **OK**.

● **NOTE**
This only works if the filters are the same throughout the selected clips. Also, if you customized filter settings between clips, they will all reset to match the settings of the first clip.

Creating a Luma Key

A Luma key allows you to key one shape into another without using an alpha channel.

In our earlier discussion of the new alpha transitions, we discovered the power of alpha channels, which contain transparency information for the image. However, black-and-white images downloaded from the Web almost never contain alpha channels.

For instance, I've found this great jigsaw puzzle piece—perfect for one of my projects as a fascinating metaphor illustrating digital complexity—but the image doesn't have an alpha channel. It's just a single-layer JPEG. How can we create a key? The answer is a Luma key.

In this example, we will key video inside the puzzle piece which is set against a black background.

1. Put the video clip to appear inside the puzzle piece on V1.

2. Put the shape directly above it on V2. In this example, I'm using a white jigsaw puzzle piece against a black background. The entire image is a single layer and saved as a JPEG.

Because the puzzle image is full-screen, it totally blocks the V1 clip below it.

3. Select the V2 clip.

4. Choose **Effects > Video Filters > Key > Luma key**. A Luma key makes portions of a clip transparent based on luminance, or grayscale, levels. Images that make great Luma keys are generally black and white, with limited shades of gray.

5. Double-click the V2 clip to load it into the Viewer, and click the **Filters** tab. Because we want to make transparent everything that's now white, select **Key Out Brighter** from the Key mode pop-up menu. (If you wanted to make the black portions transparent, use **Key Out Darker** instead)

6. Switch the View pop-up to **Matte** and adjust both the Threshold and Tolerance until you get clean edges on your key.

7. Choose **Final** from the View pop-up menu and you're done!

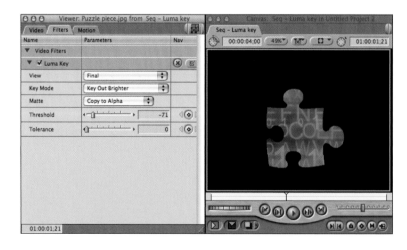

Add Burned-In Timecode to Your Sequence
Burn timecode into your sequence clips in no time flat!

Need to output a sequence with burned-in timecode matching your sequence for clients or producers to review? Piece of cake. You'll find two timecode filters when you choose **Effects > Video Filters > Video**.

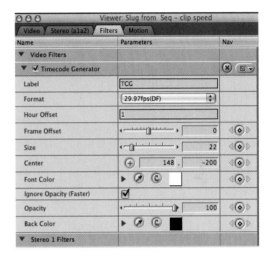

Timecode Reader displays the timecode of your source material as it was shot by the camera. This filter can be dropped directly on a clip or clips in the Timeline. Timecode Reader only shows the original timecode from your source video, so the numbers change between clips.

Timecode Generator creates timecode from zero, or a preset start time such as 01:00:00:00, that starts from the beginning of the clip to which you apply it. The most useful way to use this filter is to display sequence timecode on the Timeline. However, if you drop Timecode Generator on a clip or range of clips, it automatically restarts timecode at the start of each clip.

Some people prefer to nest the clips—which does work—however, I discovered a faster way that doesn't involve nesting.

Open the Video tab of the Viewer, and select **Generator > Slug** from the pop-up menu in the lower right. This is a clip of black audio and video. However, *before* editing the slug into the Timeline, change its duration to the length of your sequence.

Edit the slug to the top track of your Timeline across your full sequence and select it. Apply

> ● **NOTE**
> Whether you nest or use the slug, you'll still need to render—which is why I prefer to use Compressor when possible because it burns timecode into the video of a clip in the background during compression.

Effects > Video Filters > Timecode Generator. Double-click the slug to load it into the Viewer, and change the settings to match your sequence timecode. Here I changed the hours to start at **01**.

Now choose **Modify > Composite Modes > Screen**. Voilà! Just render and output.

Sharpening Your Stills
Add more focus to stills.

Looking to add a bit of "snap" to a still image? Try using the Unsharp filter.

Be cautious adding sharpening your video—most inexpensive cameras already apply sharpening during recording to improve the apparent focus of an image by making the edges more visible.

To change the less-than-optimal default settings for this filter, choose **Effects > Video Filters > Sharpen > Unsharp Mask**. Then, set Amount to **75**, Radius to **0.5**, and Threshold to **0**.

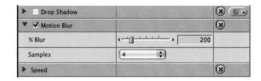

> ● **NOTE**
> Unsharp Mask, even though it has a weird name, is the best filter in the bunch to use. Don't use Sharpen, since it doesn't work as well.

> ● **NOTE**
> In the low resolution of video, sharpening can help. But don't use too much, or your edges will look harsh and could cause flicker.

Fixing Fluorescent Flicker
Ceiling fixtures driving you nuts? Try this!

You can fix fluorescent flicker showing up in your videos by opening your clip in the Viewer and selecting the **Motion Blur** option. Then, set the pop-up menu to **4** samples at **200%**.

As your shots get more complex—for example, in footage where the people featured move a lot—duplicate the track, with motion blur on the lower track, no effect on the top track, and a garbage matte to isolate the portion of the frame with a lot of movement.

Since the flicker is isolated to the small section where there is a lot of motion, it isn't as noticeable as when the entire frame flickers.

This technique generally avoids smeary video.

> ● **NOTE**
> To learn how to do garbage mattes, check out the Apple manual or my Web site.

> ● **NOTE**
> Motion Blur takes forever to render. Apply this effect only to clips that really need it.

When to Deinterlace
Deinterlacing should never be your first choice.

NTSC, PAL, and some HD formats (those that end with the letter *i*) are interlaced. This is not a bad thing—in fact, it's how the formats were designed. So, if you are creating footage for an NTSC or PAL project, it should be interlaced.

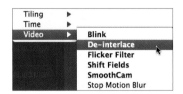

The problem is that the computer screen always displays images as progressive. This causes problems when you are editing video destined for the TV screen but watching it on the computer screen.

The problem with deinterlacing is that it cuts the vertical resolution of your image in half, making the image appear soft, with lots of fine detail getting lost. Because video doesn't have a lot of detail to start with, deinterlacing only makes matters worse.

Here are some things to keep in mind for great-looking images:

- All still images are progressive. You don't need to deinterlace a still image. If you are getting edge flickering, **Effects > Video Filters > Video > Flicker Filter** will be a better choice.

- If you are creating freeze frames for export to Photoshop, deinterlace in Photoshop, not Final Cut.

- If you are creating freeze frames in Final Cut Pro for Final Cut Pro, try to find a still that doesn't have motion and don't deinterlace it. If it flickers, then deinterlace.

- 24 fps material is always progressive and

doesn't need deinterlacing.

- If you are creating video in After Effects or other software, export the video to match your sequence settings. This means exporting interlaced DV for your DV sequence.

- If you are creating material for the Web, if possible shoot a progressive format. If not, deinterlace during compression, not during editing.

- Check your delivery specs. If you are expected to deliver an interlaced program, avoid deinterlacing as much as possible.

- The default settings for the deinterlace filters in both Final Cut Pro and Photoshop are generally correct.

As long as you remember that deinterlacing reduces image quality, and that many TV sets are designed to handle interlacing with no problems, you know enough to make the right decision most of the time.

Making Clips Black and White
Nothing says old and stylish like black and white.
Go back in time with one mouse click.

Looking to create a retro black-and-white effect on your color images?

To make a clip black and white:

1. Select the clip in the Timeline.
2. Choose **Effects > Video Filters > Image Control > Desaturate**.

Ta-da! Instant Fred Astaire and Ginger Rogers!

● **NOTE**
Desaturate provides a slider that you can adjust to remove some, but not all, of the color. This is used a lot in fashion photography to give a cool, refined look to a clip.

Creating Sepia-Toned Clips
Sepia is even better than black and white for aging a clip. Here's how.

Want to create a clip with a warm, brown tone? If you're looking for the nostalgia of a sepia-toned clip, start where the last Power Skill ended. Apply the **Desaturate** filter. This removes all the color from a clip, which gives the Sepia filter a solid base to work from.

Then, select the clip and choose **Effects > Video Filters > Image Control > Sepia**. Change the amount to around **66%**

Tweak the settings by decreasing the amount and darkening the sepia color, and you'll achieve just the effect you're looking for.

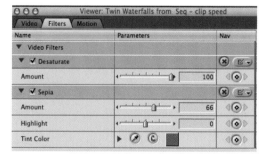

● **NOTE**
This may work best if you color-correct the clip to adjust black levels. The sepia color is applied more to the darker shades of the image.

Using the RT Menu for Scopes
The controls for your video scopes are hidden, unless you know where to look.

The video scopes in Final Cut are hidden, but you can display them in two ways: **Tools > Video Scopes**, or **Window > Arrange > Color Correction**. Of the two, I recommend the second approach.

The reason is that using the Window command realigns your screen so that you can see all five windows.

What you may not know is that when the scopes are displayed, hidden menu choices appear in the RT menu, located in the top-left corner of the Timeline.

Scope Display is a new category:

All Lines means that every pixel in every line of your clip is displayed in the scope. This is a change from earlier versions where not all pixels were displayed in the scope.

All Lines Except Top & Bottom means that every pixel in every line except the top nine and bottom nine lines is displayed. This is useful if you have closed captioning or other technical data embedded in the video signal that you want to exclude from the scopes.

Limited Lines: This displays every pixel on 32 lines of video distributed evenly within the Action Safe area.

When playing back, the real-time display always shows Limited Lines. The scope updates to full display when the playhead is paused.

> ● **NOTE**
> The lower-right corner of the video scope display indicates your video format and format choice.

Rules for Color Correction
Color correction is a huge topic; keep some basic rules in mind.

Books have been written about color correction, and we hardly scratch the surface here. Here are some useful rules.

The Waveform monitor tells us everything we need to know about the black, gray, and white in an image, but nothing about color.

The Vectorscope tells us everything we need to know about the color in an image, but nothing about black and white. We need to use these two scopes together to make sense of our image.

When color-correcting an image:

1. Never color-correct without using video scopes and a calibrated video monitor. Your computer monitor does not display color information accurately.

2. Changing color has no impact on contrast. Contrast—that is, the black, white, and gray-scale levels—must be set first.

3. The order in which you set contrast makes a difference. Set black levels to 0%. Set white levels so that they don't exceed 100%.

4. Black, white, or gray always contains equal amounts of red, green, and blue. However, saying this same thing another way is the essence of color correction: If something is supposed to be black, white, or gray, it *must* contain equal amounts of red, green, and blue.

5. To remove a color, add the opposite color.

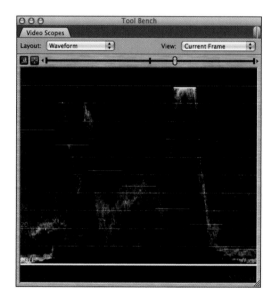

● **EXTRA CREDIT**

The best color correction filter to use is the Color Corrector 3-Way filter. You can do amazing things with it in Final Cut Pro, so consider using it before moving projects to Color.

Color-Correcting with One Mouse Click

This won't make you a colorist, but it will solve color problems in a big hurry!

Have you ever been in a hurry to meet a deadline only to discover that the camera operator forgot to color-balance the camera and everything is gold or blue? While it would be great to carefully color-balance each shot, you have exactly three nanoseconds to get this project done.

Here's a single mouse click solution that can easily fix a badly off-color image:

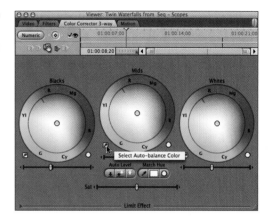

1. Put your playhead in the middle of the clip you want to color-correct.

2. Select the clip.

3. Choose **Effects > Video Filters > Color Correction > Color Corrector 3-Way**.

4. Double-click the clip to load it into the Viewer.

5. Click the **Color Corrector 3-Way** tab at the top of the Viewer.

6. Click the small eyedropper to the lower left of the Mids color wheel.

7. Click something in the image that is supposed to be pure gray.

Fixed.

● **NOTE**

Be careful not to click something that is overexposed (blown out) or that has lots of reflections.

● **NOTE**

Mid-tone grays carry the most color and are the best choice for color correction. But if there are no mid-tone grays in your shot, a good second choice is white. Just click the eyedropper to the left of the Whites color wheel and click something near white in the image.

Skin Tone Settings for Scopes
Everyone is different, but....

Each of us is an individual. However, when it comes to video, our eyes have been conditioned to expect certain colors. Our brains are programmed to recognize three colors: blue sky, green grass, and skin tone. If there is more than about a two- to three-degree difference between what we see versus what we expect, our brains tell us there's something wrong.

Use the following suggestions when you are trying to make people look "normal," or correct for a color cast in the camera.

- Caucasian skin
  - 45–70% grayscale on the Waveform monitor
  - Saturation around the second circle (40%) of the Vectorscope
- Asian/Hispanic skin
  - 35–50% gray scale on the Waveform monitor
  - Saturation between the first and second circle (30%) of the Vectorscope
- Black skin
  - 20–45% grayscale on the Waveform monitor
  - Saturation around the first circle (20%) of the Vectorscope

NOTE

These numbers assume the subject is well lit using standard studio lighting.

Keyframing the Color Corrector 3-Way Filter

This works just like it does in any other filter—once you get to the right place.

You can easily use keyframes in the Color Corrector 3-Way filter in Final Cut Pro, provided you set an initial keyframe first.

To do this:

1. Select the clip in your sequence and choose **Effects > Video Filters > Color Correction > Color Corrector 3-Way**.

2. Double-click the clip in your sequence to load it into the Viewer.

3. Put your playhead in the clip in the Timeline where you want to set your first keyframe.

4. Select the **Color Corrector 3-Way** tab at the top of the Viewer and click the keyframe diamond at the top of the filter.

5. Move the playhead to the next position and adjust a setting. Since you have already applied a keyframe to every parameter in the effect, making any adjustments later automatically sets a new keyframe for that parameter.

● **EXTRA CREDIT**

If you want to see your keyframes, adjust them individually, or delete them, click the **Numeric** button in the top-left corner of the filter. To return to the visual display, click the Visual button.

Fix It Before You Start
Normally, you color-correct at the end.
With multiclips, color-correct at the start.

You're about to edit a music video using multiclips, but one camera was not properly color balanced. Normally, you'd fix this at the end of the production—which would mean color-correcting the same clip dozens of times. You could copy and paste the filter into multiple clips, but there's a better way.

Edit the source clip—before you build the master clip—into the Timeline and color-correct it as you would normally. When you are happy with the look of the clip, double-click the clip to be sure it is loaded into the Viewer. Drag the **Color Corrector 3-Way** filter from the Filters tab into the Browser. This adds the filter to the list of clips in the Browser.

Load the source clip from the Browser into the Viewer, and then drop the filter setting you stored in the Browser onto the clip in the Viewer. This applies the color correction setting to the source clip.

Now when you create your multiclip, the color correction filter will travel with the clip into the multiclip. Although you won't see it as you edit the multiclip in the Viewer, when you play the Timeline the filter will be applied automatically.

> **● NOTE**
>
> This technique works with any filter or motion effect. If you don't need to see the results of the filter settings prior to building the multiclip, simply load your Browser clip into the Viewer and apply the effect. Because color correction requires adjusting the filter in the Viewer while viewing it in the Canvas and checking the scopes, we needed to add the step of dragging the filter settings to the Browser. You can't apply a filter by dragging it on top of a clip in the Browser.

Color-Correcting a Sudden Color Change
Here's a faster way to quickly compensate for an
unintended color shift during a scene.

While keyframing the Color Corrector filter gives us lots of control, it also takes a long time. In looking for a faster way to fix a problem, such as when the talent walks outside—out of tungsten light into daylight—Lee Berger suggests this tip.

Instead of keyframing, split the clip at the change in lighting using the **Razor** tool (press **B**).

Apply the Color Corrector 3-Way filter to each clip, and then color-correct each clip as necessary. Apply a dissolve to the split point.

This trick makes it easy to shift or extend the transition point without having to deal with keyframes.

Monitoring Video Levels
Final Cut Pro provides a fast way to check your video levels.

In the Audio chapter, we learned that there are three technical requirements in every project: audio levels that don't distort, video white levels below 100 percent, and video chroma levels that are not excessive.

Keeping white levels below 100 percent and chroma levels from oversaturating is a key part of the finishing process of your video. The video scopes help, but there is an additional tool you can use that makes monitoring video levels very easy.

Final Cut Pro includes an indicator you can use to check video white levels. It's called Range Check, and you access it by choosing **View > Range Check > Excess Luma**.

To use it, put your playhead in the clip you want to check and press **Control+Z**. This checks that frame for white levels. If your white levels are between 90 and 100 percent, a green check box with an up-pointing arrow is displayed (left). If your white levels exceed 100 percent, a yellow warning is displayed (center). If your white levels are 90 percent or below, a green check box alone appears (right.)

You can use a similar tool to test chroma levels. Choose **View > Range Check > Excess Chroma**. There are only two indicators here: a green check box indicates your chroma levels are OK; yellow indicates you have problems.

You can also choose **View > Range Check > Both**, except that the indicator doesn't specify whether the problem is white levels or chroma levels. For this reason, I use the Luma Check first, followed by Chroma Check.

Finally, you adjust video level settings using the Color Corrector 3-Way filter.

● **NOTE**

While this check box is not as accurate as a $15,000 Tektronix video scope, you'll find that you can trust it in most situations.

● **EXTRA CREDIT**

This display does not update in real time, which is a real shame, because if it did, you could watch your show and your video levels at the same time. However, a great workaround is **Option+P**. This will play your sequence in close to real time, while still displaying the Range Check.

Keep Your White Levels Broadcast Safe
White levels over 100 percent are a sure way to disaster. Read this.

When editing in Final Cut Pro, take precautions to keep your white levels "broadcast safe."

Digital white can be recorded with levels as high as 109 percent, but any level above 100 percent is too high for the analog world of video. Excess white levels can cause visual breakup, transmitter overmodulation, audio buzz, and angry finger-pointing. Even in today's digital world, this is still an issue for any images distributed via DVDs or displayed via down-conversion on older analog TVs.

Most of the time, you'll control your white levels using the Color Corrector 3-Way filter. However, sometimes there's a lack of time, or a specular needs some fast clamping. Final Cut prevents excess white levels on imported graphics and images automatically, but it does not do so for video.

Color Correction ▶	Broadcast Safe
Distort ▶	Color Corrector
Glow ▶	Color Corrector 3-way
Image Control ▶	Desaturate Highlights
Key ▶	Desaturate Lows
Matte ▶	RGB Balance
Nattress Film Effects ▶	RGB Limit

● **NOTE**

The default settings for the Broadcast Safe filter are fine. You don't need to make any adjustments. In fact, Apple recommends against changing them.

When you need to be absolutely sure your white levels are safe, apply the Broadcast Safe filter by choosing **Effects > Video Filters > Color Correction > Broadcast Safe**.

The Twirling Thingy of Color
It's a curved arrow that seems to do absolutely nothing, except...

...help you when you need to pick a color.

The eyedropper on the left allows you to select a color from anywhere on your screen, not just from within a clip. The color chip on the right allows you to select a color using a variety of color pickers. However, when you click this middle color whatsit, the only thing that seems to happen is that the arrow changes direction. What the heck is it?

This color twirly button determines the direction of color rotation as you use keyframes to change

colors. For instance, if it points clockwise, the colors rotate from green to red to blue and back to green. If it points counterclockwise, the colors rotate in the opposite direction, from green to blue to red and back to green.

Now you know.

CHAPTER 8

Export and Output

It's time for the final stage. With editing and effects complete, we need to get our project out of Final Cut Pro so the world can see it.

In the past, most projects would output to tape. Today the majority of projects are outputting to files—files that post to the Web, are placed on a DVD, or are broadcast via a playout server at the network.

The latest version of Final Cut Studio reflects this trend. Apple made few changes to their ability to output to tape, but they totally overhauled and improved exporting.

In this chapter, we'll take a look at some of the less-obvious techniques you can use to get your projects out of Final Cut Pro and send them on their way.

Share the Good News
Final Cut Pro 7 offers sharing.

The two biggest problems with exporting from previous versions of Final Cut were that it took forever and unless you had a degree in rocket science you could never be sure your settings were correct. In any case, you were rarely happy with the results.

Apple fixed both these problems with Share in Final Cut Pro 7. Share is a one-stop system for compressing and publishing your files based on a set of prebuilt templates that Apple provides.

The biggest news with Share is that it runs in the background. This means that you can export a project while editing it at the same time. In fact, you can even be editing the exact same project you are exporting.

The other news is that Share only outputs one Timeline sequence to one destination. But there's a big workaround: the Browser. Before selecting Share, go into the Browser and select one clip, a range of clips, a bin, a range of bins, a sequence, or a range of sequences.

Share will build these into your choice of separate sources, or one large clip. And, if you select one large clip, Share can add Chapter markers at the start of each clip that transfer into the exported QuickTime movie, standard DVD, or Blu-ray Disc.

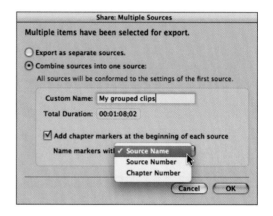

NOTE

Contrary to what you might think, Share does not allow multiple users to share the same files. Instead, it allows you to easily share your files with others.

Send To Compressor
Sometimes, Share isn't enough.

The benefit of using Share is that it is fast and easy. However, it isn't flexible. All the settings are fixed. If you need to customize your compression settings, that's where Send to Compressor comes in.

You can Send files to Compressor in two ways:

- From the Share window (**File > Share**)
- From the File menu (**File > Send To > Compressor**)

The benefits to using the Share window are that you can apply a compression preset and destination setting to all your files before sending them to Compressor. This saves time configuring them in Compressor.

The benefit to using **File > Send To > Compressor** is that you bypass the Share window, which means exports start faster.

In both cases, exporting happens in the background and the export quality is determined by the settings you use. If the settings are the same, the quality will be the same.

> **NOTE**
> You can also access the Send to Compressor option by Control-clicking a clip in the Timeline or Browser.

Accessing Custom Compressor Presets from Share
You aren't locked into Share's presets—provided you know where to look.

The simplicity of Share is that you have a limited number of choices to make. You pick the preset and click **Export**. But what if you want to add a watermark, or scale the image to a different size. You can't modify Share's presets. Does that mean you are out of luck?

No, you just need to look a bit deeper into the Share window. The bottom choice in the Preset pop-up is **Custom**. Select this, and the Settings window from Compressor is displayed.

Here you can select from any Apple preset for Compressor, *or* choose any custom setting you previously created and saved. This means that unless you need to modify a preset, you don't need to go into Compressor, as you can access all your settings from the Share menu.

● **EXTRA CREDIT**

When displaying the Custom Setting menu, select the **Menu** check box and your custom Compressor setting shows up in the Share Preset pop-up menu.

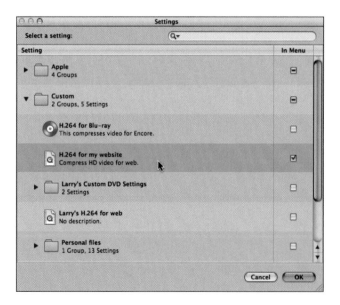

Share vs. Send vs. Export
Four ways to export your files—which should you pick?

If you have an earlier version of Final Cut Pro, your best export option is **File > Export > Quick-Time Movie**. So that decision is easy. With Final Cut Pro 7, other choices appear.

File > Share provides a fast way to assign a compression setting and destination for one or more files. It can build all your selected files into a single master movie or output them as separate files. However, it limits you to one destination per share window and requires a preset compression setting.

File > Send to Compressor is the best choice when you want to create a customized compression setting that you have not yet saved as a preset. It is also the best choice when you want to send a file or files to multiple destinations.

Both Send and Share do their exporting in the background, making them very fast. Actually, the exporting process still takes a long time, but since Final Cut Pro is ready for you to continue editing almost immediately after you click Export, these give you the appearance of exporting instantly. Don't be surprised if your compressed files take a while to appear.

Share...	⇧⌘E	Hummingbirds CU 03
Export	▶	QuickTime Movie...　⌘E
Send To	▶	Using QuickTime Conversion...
Batch Export		

> ● **NOTE**
>
> When you Send a file to Compressor using a destination of Source, the compressed file will be stored at the root level of your startup disk.

File > Export > QuickTime Movie is the fastest way to get your movie out of Final Cut Pro. This approach is best used when you need a stand-alone file with outstanding image quality. Use this when you want to create a master file you can store, transfer to another computer, or process separately through Compressor.

File > Export > Using QuickTime Conversion is the best choice for exporting freeze frames or compressing video using third-party software that doesn't work with Compressor.

Batch Export: Is It Still Worth Doing?

Yes, Batch Export still has its uses.

With the advent of Share, does Batch Export still make sense? In short, yes. Batch Export is particularly useful when you have a lot of clips or sequences to export at once, or if you need to export the same sequence to multiple formats and settings. You can select as many clips, bins, and sequences as you need to export. Exported items are grouped into batches. It is the batch that determines the export setting, rather than the clips in it.

To use Batch Export:

1. Select the items—clips, bins, sequences—you want to export.

2. Choose **File > Batch Export**. Notice that all your selected items are grouped into the same bin. All items in the same batch export with the same settings.

3. Repeat this process as necessary. Each group of selected files is placed into a new batch every time you select **File > Batch Export**.

4. Select a Batch folder in the Batch Export window.

5. Click the **Settings** button.

6. Adjust the export settings as necessary for each batch.

7. When all batches are configured, click **Export** to start the process.

● **NOTE**

Items that you place in the Batch Export Queue disappear when you quit Final Cut. If that happens, you'll need to rebatch them when you restart the program.

● **EXTRA CREDIT**

You can drag files from one batch to another. Also, you can delete files from a batch by highlighting the file and pressing **Delete**, and you can make a copy of a file by **Option-dragging**.

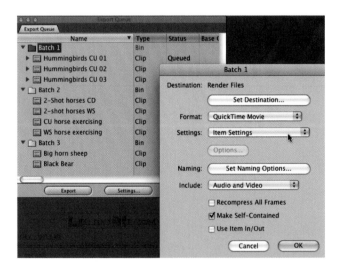

Creating a Blu-ray Disc
There are two ways to record Blu-ray media.
Here's how to decide.

With the latest release of Final Cut Pro, Apple is taking the first tentative steps to supporting Blu-ray. In fact, Final Cut Pro, via Share, can now create Blu-ray Discs. Sort of...

Blu-ray is two things: a format for compressing high-definition video and a format for storing those compressed files onto optical media. Currently the Macintosh operating system does not support playing back Blu-ray Discs—which means that you need to purchase a separate Blu-ray player, such as a Sony PlayStation 3, in order to view the discs you create.

However, there are two ways to burn a Blu-ray Disc: using existing DVD burners, such as a SuperDrive, or using Blu-ray burners. Apple calls Blu-ray media burned to a standard DVD an AVCHD (Advanced Video Codec High Definition) disc. Only Blu-ray media burned to a Blu-ray Disc can be called a Blu-ray Disc.

The good news about AVCHD discs is that you can burn them, but not view them, on your current DVD burner. They don't hold as much media—30–60 minutes worth—nor does it have the same quality as Blu-ray Disc because the AVCHD disc doesn't support the same high data rate. However, Apple has done a great job in optimizing the compression settings to make the Blu-ray media you create look really good.

So, if you are looking for an easy way to create high-def discs, AVCHD is the way to go.

● **EXTRA CREDIT**

To configure the interface settings for a high-def disc, click **Create Blu-ray Disc** when selecting the Blu-ray option in Share.

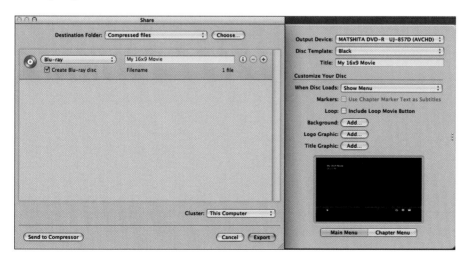

Send To vs. Open In Editor
How do you decide which to use?

When you want to send a file from Final Cut Pro to another application, you have two choices: Send To, or Open in Editor.

You use **Send To** when you are sending a file that was created in Final Cut Pro to another application for the first time. For instance, you use it to send a clip that was captured in Final Cut to Motion.

You use **Open in Editor** when you are opening a file that was created in another application. For instance, you use Open in Editor when you have a Motion project edited to the Final Cut Pro Timeline that you want to return to Motion to make changes.

Examples of files that you use Open in Editor for include:

- Motion projects
- Soundtrack audio projects
- Soundtrack multitrack projects
- Photoshop PSD files
- LiveType files

Here's an easy way to think of this: The first time, you *Send* it; after that, you *Open* it.

You Don't Need to Run Compressor to Compress
Strange, but true!

Compressor isn't used to compress a clip. Just like Share, Compressor is used to determine the compression settings for a clip, then it hands the file over to another program to compress the file.

The actual compression is done by an application with no user interface called a daemon. (Daemons are Unix files that run invisibly in the background.)

So, once you submit a file for compressing, you can safely—and with a clear conscience—quit Compressor.

● **NOTE**
Batch Monitor is just a monitor for the compression process. You don't need to have it running to compress, either.

● **EXTRA CREDIT**
If you want to see how hard your computer is working to compress your video, choose **Utilities > Activity Monitor**, choose **Window > Activity Monitor,** and click the **CPU** tab.

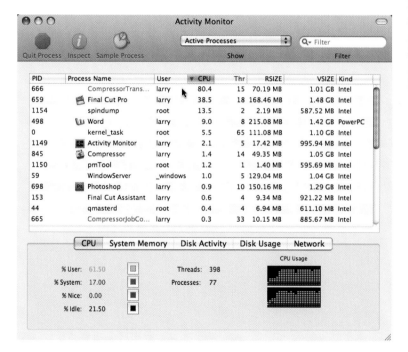

Exporting Freeze Frames
Final Cut Pro makes it easy to export a freeze frame.

You don't need to create the freeze frames, also called "still frames," first. Here are the steps:

1. Park your playhead on the frame you want to export. This can be in the Viewer, Canvas, or Timeline.

2. Choose **File > Export > Using QuickTime Conversion**.

3. Select **Still Image** from the Format menu at the bottom.

4. Leave Use set to **Default Settings**.

5. The default export format for still images is PNG, which is an uncompressed image format. Leave this setting alone as it is a good choice for stills.

6. Give the image a name and location where you want it saved.

7. Click **Save**.

> **NOTE**
> Final Cut Pro version 6.0.2 had a bug with image exporting. Upgrading to a later version fixes it.

> **NOTE**
> Don't deinterlace your images in Final Cut Pro before exporting. As you'll read in a moment, Photoshop does a much better job.

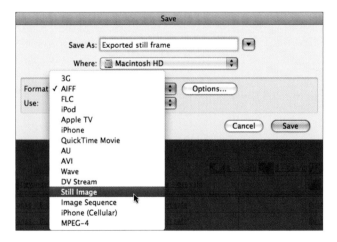

Exporting a Batch of Freeze Frames
Here's a fast way to export a collection of still images.

Follow these steps:

1. Create a bin in the Browser to store your images. Call it, for example, Images.

2. Put your playhead on the frame you want to freeze, either in the Viewer or the Timeline, and select **Modify > Make Freeze Frame** (or press **Shift+N**). This creates a freeze frame and displays it in the Viewer.

3. Drag the freeze frame from the Viewer to your newly created Images bin in the Browser. In the Browser, remove the timecode reference from the end of the filename. The colons in the timecode will prevent it from exporting.

4. Continue this process until you have collected all the images you desire in this bin. Make sure all filenames are unique and all colons are removed.

5. Select all the images in the bin and choose **File > Batch Export**.

6. Select the Batch folder and click **Settings**.

7. Set Format to **Still Image**.

8. Set Destination to the destination of your choice.

9. The defaults for Options and Naming should be fine, so leave them alone.

10. Set Settings to **Default Settings** and click **OK**.

11. Click **Export**, and you're done!

Resizing Exported Freeze Frames

Exported video freeze frames look stretched. Here's how to fix them.

Just as we need to prep our images to look good for importing, we also need to adjust video freeze frames after exporting from Final Cut. The reason is that most video uses rectangular pixels for images while the computer uses square pixels.

NOTE

Once you correct for the aspect ratio, you can continue to scale the image size as much as you want.

Import your video freeze frames into Photoshop, and then follow these steps:

1. Deinterlace your image (choose **Filters > Video > Deinterlace**). The default deinterlace settings are fine. Photoshop does a much better job deinterlacing than Final Cut Pro does.

2. Adjust your image quality as necessary. Add any other effects you want.

3. As the last step, correct the aspect ratio by resizing your image according to the following table. (Remember to turn off **Constrain Proportions** and set Resolution to **72**.)

RESIZING FREEZE FRAMES

Video Format	Aspect Ratio	Resize Freeze Frame to
DV NTSC	4:3	640 x 480
DV NTSC	16:9	720 x 405
SD NTSC	4:3	640 x 480
SD NTSC	16:9	720 x 405
PAL	4:3	768 x 576
PAL	16:9	1024 x 576
HD 720	16:9	1280 x 720
HD 1080	16:9	1920 x 1080

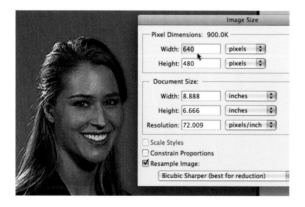

When to Deinterlace

Just because you can see the lines doesn't mean you should get rid of them.

Interlacing was invented at the dawn of television, back in the 1930s, to solve a variety of technical issues. Since that day, all NTSC and PAL footage is interlaced. The TV you've been watching all your life is interlaced. There is nothing inherently wrong with interlacing. It is built into the design of the format. Even today, some HD footage is interlaced—all the formats that end with the letter *i*, for example. Even some of our networks transmit interlaced HD images—CBS, NBC, and PBS, to name three.

However, a problem arises as we start to watch programs designed for the TV set on our computer. TVs are interlaced. Computers are not. TVs don't show interlace lines. Computers do.

One way to get around this problem is to shoot everything in progressive (non-interlaced) mode. However, not all cameras support this format and even some that say they do, don't.

Before you decide to deinterlace all your footage, keep in mind that deinterlacing essentially removes every other horizontal line in your image. At best you lose detail; at worst, your image starts looking soft.

Here are some basic rules of thumb:

- If your program is going to be principally viewed on a TV, don't deinterlace.
- If your program is going to be viewed on a computer, compress the image size to 50 percent of the original size or smaller. This retains your image quality while making interlacing disappear.
- If you are shooting an image to be projected to a large screen (i.e., theaters), shoot progressive. Nothing you do with interlacing is going to improve your image.
- *Don't* deinterlace freeze frames that you plan to export, prior to exporting.
- *Don't* deinterlace freeze frames that you are editing back into your sequence unless they are flickering.
- Deinterlacing has no effect on flickering lines within still images. Use the flicker filter instead.
- Triple-check that your camera actually shoots a progressive image. Don't believe the manufacturer's marketing blurb.

EDL vs. XML
Which should you use when moving a project between systems?

The EDL (Edit Decision List) was invented more than 25 years ago as a way to store sequence edit information. In those days, we edited between analog reels of tape using very expensive tape deck controllers, like CMX systems. Since then, EDLs have been used to simplify the process of moving video projects between systems, such as between Avid and Final Cut Pro.

The problem with EDLs is that they are very limited—they only support two tracks of video and a maximum of four tracks of audio, depending on the EDL format you select. Outputting complex sequences requires creating multiple EDLs.

Worse, when using EDLs, different editing systems treat Reel IDs differently. (Accurate Reel IDs are essential to recapturing source footage, which is mandatory with EDL transfers.) Avid allows up to 15 characters but only allows the first 8 characters to be unique. Final Cut permits Reel IDs to contain only 6 characters when using the CMX 3600 format.

Even worse, not all frame rates are supported, which means you could shoot a project that an EDL won't export. Much more robust format exchange languages are XML (Extensible Markup Language) for Final Cut Pro and AAF (Advanced Authoring Format) for Avid.

In general, use an EDL to move a project when you are early in the edit process, before applying any effects or sophisticated transition effects. Otherwise, XML is a much better choice—especially when used in conjunction with Automatic Duck software.

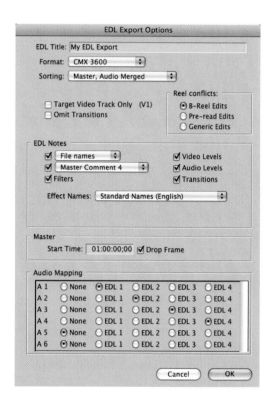

● **NOTE**

Automatic Duck is an excellent and very popular tool to move projects between editing applications; learn more at www.automaticduck.com.

Go Back to the Past with XML

XML solves the problem of converting a project to an earlier version.

Final Cut makes it easy to bring an older project into a newer version of the software. Just open the file and Final Cut converts it automatically.

However, how do you move a later project back to an earlier version? By using XML—here's how:

1. In the older version of Final Cut, choose **File > Export > XML** and make note of the highest level of XML that version supports. Final Cut Pro 6, for instance, supports XML version 4, while Final Cut Pro 5 supports XML version 3.

2. Return to the newer version of Final Cut Pro, and in the Browser, select the sequence, bins, and/or clips you want to move back to the earlier version.

3. Choose **File > Export > XML**. From the Format pop-up menu, select the highest version of XML which is supported in the *older* version of Final Cut Pro.

4. Leave the remaining settings at their default and click **OK**.

5. Copy the XML file to the other, older, system.

6. In the older system, choose **File > Import > XML**, then select the XML file you transferred from the newer system.

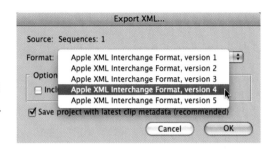

NOTE

Features in the newer version of Final Cut that are not supported on the older system, such as filters or speed effects, will be ignored. If the media is not on the older system, you will need to transfer it manually. XML contains pointers to the media, not the media itself. If the media format is not supported by the earlier version of Final Cut Pro, you will need to recapture it in a format that is supported.

NOTE

When converting a project from an older version, Final Cut Pro doesn't make the conversion permanent until you save the file. So, if you don't save the file in the newer version, you will still be able to open it with the earlier version.

Using XML to Move Favorite Effects
Here's how to move effects between projects when Copy/Paste won't work.

Want to move your favorite effect settings from project to project? Easy. Use Copy and Paste; or just drag and drop.

But what if those projects are on different computers thousands of miles apart? Try this XML workaround instead.

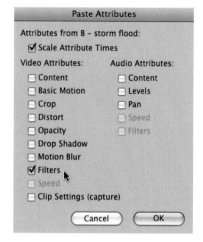

1. In the project that contains the effects you want to move, create a new sequence.

2. From the Video Generators pop-up menu in the lower-right corner of the Viewer, create a slug (a clip consisting of audio and video black). The length of the slug is not important, unless you're using keyframes to time an effect.

3. Edit the slug into a new sequence.

4. Create a slug for every effect you want to move.

5. Select a clip with an effect setting that you want to move and press **Command+C**.

6. Select the first slug and choose **Edit > Paste Attributes**.

7. Drag the slug to the Browser and give it an identifying name. Repeat this process until all effects have been copied to slugs and all slugs are named and in the Browser.

8. Select all your effects slugs in the Browser and export them using XML (choose **File > Export > XML**).

9. Transfer the XML file to the new computer and open the project in which you want to import the effects.

10. Select **File > Import > XML**.

Your effects now show up as clips in the Browser. You can keep them in the Browser, drag them to your Favorites folder, or use **Edit > Paste Attributes** to apply them to clips in your Timeline.

Exporting Lists for Excel
Here's an easy way to get data out of Final Cut Pro and into Excel.

If you want a quick reference of all your clip info, but you don't want to open Final Cut Pro and wait for it to load your project every time, consider exporting your logging information into Excel. When you have hours and hours of material, this can be a great way to access and share data quickly—especially for systems that aren't running Final Cut.

Follow these steps:

1. Open the Final Cut Pro project that has the clips with the information you want to export.

2. Select the Browser.

3. Choose **File > Export > Batch List**.

4. Name your file, choose a destination (the Desktop works well for this), and select **Tabbed Text** for the format.

5. Open Excel.

6. Drag the file from the Desktop onto the Excel icon in your Dock. (Double-clicking the file will open it in Final Cut Pro, which we don't want.)

7. Excel opens it, and very cleverly puts each clip in its own row, neatly duplicating all the Browser columns in your worksheet.

> **NOTE**
> Intelligent Assistance recently released several pieces of utility software that make this process a lot more flexible. Learn more at www.intelligentassistance.com.

> **NOTE**
> Exporting a batch list exports everything in the Browser. There is no way to restrict the export to a selection of clips or range of columns.

Exporting Marker Lists
Exporting marker information is now a piece of cake.

With the release of Final Cut Pro 7, we can now export marker data as a tab-delimited text file. This allows us to analyze, format, search, print, and share marker data.

Here's how:

1. Select the sequence or clips you want to export.
2. Choose **File > Export > Markers List as Text**.
3. In the Save dialog box, give the file a name and destination.
4. From the pop-up menu, select which types of markers you want to export.
5. Click **Save**.

NOTE

This option is grayed out if you select multiple clips in the Browser.

NOTE

Marker fields that are exported include Sequence Name, Marker Type, Marker Name, Comment, Start Timecode, Duration, and Color.

	A	B	C	D	E	F	G
1	Name	Type	Marker Name	Comment	Start	Duration	Color
2	Seq - markers	Sequence	Music start	Need soft, tenuous feeling	01:00:06;17	00:00:00;00	Orange
3	Seq - markers	Sequence	Music end		01:00:29;12	00:00:00;00	Orange
4	Seq - markers	Sequence	Color correct	Emphasize gold in sky	01:00:46;22	00:00:00;00	Red
5	Hummingbird Sunset	Clip	Female in sunlight		01:00:51;29	00:00:00;00	Blue
6	Hummingbird Nest	Clip	Bird lands		01:00:14;24	00:00:00;00	Orange
7	Hummingbird in flight	Clip	Male hovers		01:00:02;06	00:00:00;00	Green

Round-Tripping Audio to Soundtrack Pro

Faster than a speeding export, this is the best way to share audio files between Final Cut Pro and Soundtrack Pro.

A faster way to work with audio in both Final Cut Pro and Soundtrack Pro is called round-tripping. You have three ways to send files:

- **Send to Audio File Project** sends a single mono, or stereo pair, audio clip to Soundtrack Pro for repair. To bring it back to Final Cut Pro, simply save the file in Soundtrack Pro. Using this option, you can send only one file at a time.

- **Send to Multitrack Project** sends a single clip, group of clips, or entire sequence to Soundtrack Pro for mixing. Recent versions of Soundtrack also support audio repair within the mixing window. To return the audio to Final Cut Pro, select **File > Export** in Soundtrack.

- **Send to Soundtrack Pro Script** modifies the source file stored on your hard disk. This option has the potential of permanently altering your master file, so use this option cautiously.

NOTE

If you select Soundtrack Pro Script and the script contains keyframes, the placement of the keyframes may change, depending on the difference in duration between the keyframes in the script and the source clip on disk.

Timecode Concerns When Exporting for DVD Subtitles

DVD subtitles are keyed to video timecode—but not the timecode you expect.

Hiring a subtitle company to create subtitles, and then importing the text file they create, is often the fastest way to get subtitles into DVD Studio Pro. However, in order for this to work, the subtitles must have a timecode reference. And that timecode needs to match the timecode of the track in DVD Studio Pro.

The problem is, the timecode of your Final Cut Pro sequence is almost always changed during compression. This means that the QuickTime movie you sent the subtitle company won't match the timecode of your compressed MPEG-2 video.

By default, when you export out of Final Cut, your timecode starts at hour 01. When you compress an MPEG-2 file, by default the timecode starts at hour 0. In other words, the timecodes don't match, which breaks the import process.

To fix this, do one of the following:

- Change the timecode references in the subtitle text file.
- Change the timecode of your Final Cut Pro sequence prior to export (choose **Sequence > Settings > Timeline Options**).
- Change the starting timecode in Compressor before you compress the file. You can change the timecode on the **Video Format** tab in Compressor's Inspector window.

You can change timecode settings at any time inside Final Cut Pro without doing damage to your project.

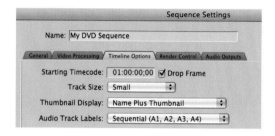

NOTE

In my experience, only the hours reference needs to change. Minutes, seconds, and frames are not a problem.

EXTRA CREDIT

Most DVDs are produced using non-drop-frame timecode. Make a point to check before exporting.

Print to Video vs. Edit to Tape
In spite of what you read, tape still exists.
Here's how to decide how to output.

There's Export—which means to create a file—and there's Output—which means to record to tape. You "output" when you want to lay your sequence off to tape. And there are two options that do this: Print to Video and Edit to Tape. Which do you use?

Choose **File > Print to Video** when you need to record to tape at high quality and you don't care what the timecode of your sequence is on the tape. Print to Video uses what's called a "dirty-in and dirty-out." This means that you have image break-up at both the In and Out points. For this reason, Print to Video should only be used for entire sequences and have plenty of black at the beginning and end of the sequence. (If I don't have bars at the beginning, I generally add 10 seconds of black at the beginning and 60 seconds of black at the end of my sequence.)

Choose **File > Edit to Tape** when you need to record to tape at high quality, and you need to record at a specific timecode on the tape. Most professional organizations require programs to start at timecode 01:00:00:00. Edit to Tape can create two edit options: an Assemble edit, which does a "clean-in and dirty-out," or an Insert edit, which does a "clean-in and clean-out." With this option, you set an In and an Out point and edit to the tape like you edit to the Timeline. For this reason, Edit to Tape is good for recording entire programs (an Assemble edit), or just "punching in" a short segment (an Insert edit).

● **NOTE**
While virtually all video tape decks support Assemble edits, not all decks support Insert edits.

● **NOTE**
There is no difference in quality between these two options. Edit to Tape requires timecode to be recorded on the tape prior to output (see the next Power Skill for more).

● **EXTRA CREDIT**
Always ask if your client needs drop-frame or timecode. Most broadcast outlets say yes; others say no. Make a point to ask. Also, many HD formats also use drop-frame timecode.

Recording Timecode to Tape

Like horseshoeing, recording timecode to tape is a vanishing art.

I couldn't resist ending a book covering the latest in technology with something from the last century—recording timecode to tape.

You need to record timecode to tape—a process called *striping*—in order to use **File > Edit to Tape**.

Depending on the capability of the tape deck, this can often be handled directly by the deck. But for those decks that don't support this, Final Cut can help.

- Connect your deck, power up, and put in a fresh blank tape.
- Start Final Cut Pro (note that you do this *after* the deck is connected and powered up).
- Choose **File > Edit to Tape**.
- In the top center, click the small black button that looks like a squashed centipede—this is the Black and Code button. (Yes, it really is that tiny. No, it doesn't appear anywhere else in the application.)
- Follow the dialog boxes that appear after you click the button.
- Recording black and code is real time. An hour tape takes an hour.

NOTE

Recording black and code will completely erase your tape. Be sure that you loaded a blank one. There is no undo here.

Index

Safari
Books Online

Get free online access to this book for 45 days!

And get access to thousands more by signing up for a free trial to Safari Books Online!

With the purchase of this book you have instant online, searchable access to it for 45 days on Safari Books Online! And while you're there, be sure to check out Safari Books Online's on-demand digital library and their free trial offer (a separate sign-up process). Safari Books Online subscribers have access to thousands of technical, creative and business books, instructional videos, and articles from the world's leading publishers.

Simply visit www.peachpit.com/safarienabled and enter code DMNNZBI to try it today.